THE CANARY TRAINER

ALSO BY NICHOLAS MEYER

Target Practice

The Seven-Per-Cent Solution

The West End Horror

Black Orchid (coauthor)

Confessions of a Homing Pigeon

Screenplays

The Seven-Per-Cent Solution

Time After Time

Company Business

Star Trek II (coauthor)

Star Trek IV (coauthor)

Star Trek VI (coauthor)

Sommersby (coauthor)

Plays

Loco Motives

T H E
Canary Trainer

From the Memoirs of
JOHN H. WATSON
as edited by
NICHOLAS MEYER

W. W. Norton & Company

New York   •   *London*

Based on the Sherlock Holmes characters created by Sir Arthur Conan Doyle

First Edition

The text of this book is composed in New Baskerville,
with the display set in Dorchester Script.
Composition and manufacturing by The Haddon Craftsmen, Inc.
Book design by Beth Tondreau Design.

LIBRARY OF CONGRESS CATALOGING-IN-PUBLICATION DATA
Meyer, Nicholas.
The canary trainer : from the memoirs of John H. Watson, M.D. / as
edited by Nicholas Meyer
p.   cm.
Sequel to: The seven-per-cent solution.
1. Holmes, Sherlock (Fictitious character)—Fiction.   2. Private
investigators—France—Paris—Fiction.   3. Opera—France—Paris—
Fiction.   4. Paris (France)—Fiction.   I. Title.
PS3563.E88C3   1993
813'.54—dc20   93–13149

ISBN 0-393-03608-1

W. W. Norton & Company, Inc., 500 Fifth Avenue, New York, N.Y. 10110
W. W. Norton & Company Ltd., 10 Coptic Street, London WC1A 1PU

1 2 3 4 5 6 7 8 9 0

for Lauren, for Rachel, and for Madeline

with all the love there is

EDITOR'S FOREWORD

Beinecke Library
Department of Special Collections
Yale University
New Haven, Connecticut

December 11, 1992

Dear Mr. Meyer:

I am assistant curator for Special Collections at the Beinecke, and I am writing to ask your advice and also your assistance.

As you may know, the Beinecke is the recipient of an enormous number of valuable papers and manuscripts from donors the world over.

Recently we have transferred our entire catalogue from an analog to a digitalized computer format in order to facilitate referencing, a process that has consumed several months (and two million dollars). Along the way, we have unearthed several documents which were not properly identified or studied at the time of their acquisition.

Among the papers on repository at the library are several pertaining to the estate of Martha Hudson, whose brother-in-law, Gerald

Forrester, was a distinguished Yale alumnus ('03). The university has been in possession of these papers for over fifty years.

I am ashamed to confess that the name Martha Hudson did not mean anything to my predecessor and so, I fear, her papers escaped the scrutiny they deserved. It was only when the digital catalogue transfer occurred that we realized that this Martha Hudson was for thirty years the housekeeper of Sherlock Holmes.

Most of Mrs. Hudson's papers are of little interest. They seem mainly to consist of housekeeping accounts that shed some light (but not much) on prices and priorities in a late-Victorian/Edwardian bachelor establishment and as such will perhaps fascinate social historians specializing in the period.

The reason I am writing you, however, is that among the Hudson papers was discovered a manuscript purporting to be by Holmes's biographer, John H. Watson. How it came to be included among Mrs. Hudson's household accounts we have no way of knowing. Possibly because the bulk of the material is in fact a transcription of a lengthy deposition by Holmes himself (i.e., her employer), there may have been some confusion as to authorship. How this resulted in her coming into possession of the manuscript we cannot explain. (Mr. Forrester himself passed on in 1953 and has no heirs who might enlighten us on the subject.)

Knowing of your past work in this field, the library wonders if you would be interested in reading, editing, and annotating the text for publication.

I will be away over the holiday but back after the new year, when I can be reached at the above address, by telephone or by fax. If we do not speak before then, have a Merry Christmas.

Sincerely,

Fred Malcolm
Assistant Curator,
Special Collections

This letter explains as well as I could how the following manu-script has come to light. I don't mean to seem churlish, but it is astonishing to me that library scholarship is in such a sorry state that a find of such potential significance should have been allowed to gather dust on the shelf of a major university for half a century. It's no damn good having piles of documents in your collection if no one bothers to read them. And it isn't a sufficient cop-out to point the finger at the Reagan and Bush administrations' attitude towards education and research and bemoan the fact that there aren't enough scholars to go round. The blame cannot simply be laid at the door of such a recent development. The stuff has been sitting there for years.

At this rate, more parts of *Huckleberry Finn, For Whom the Bell Tolls,* and goodness knows what else are still destined to languish unpublished—not in someone's attic, which I could understand, but in the very precincts of academia that are supposed to protect and preserve them for the rest of us.

Enough.

A few words about the manuscript itself.

Since the discovery of the so-called Swingline-Dobson text in 1970, an entire cottage industry of "newly discovered" Watsonian manuscripts has cluttered the field of Sherlockian scholarship. Some may well be authentic, others palpably are not. Enthusiastic perpetrators are second in their creative zeal only to Howard Hughes's autobiographers and those writing entries into Hitler's diaries.

The chief problem posed by any Watsonian text must, of course, be the question of authenticity. In the case of the present manuscript, known as *The Canary Trainer,* the question of prove-nance is complicated by a number of factors.

First, although the paper and ink conform to the proper time

and place and the manuscript itself appears to be indisputably written in Watson's hand* (on a rather bumpy surface), this is not a case in which Watson appears as either a witness or a participant. Watson's text was seemingly dictated in whole or part by Holmes himself, which greatly confuses the issue of authorial voice, one of the crucial methods by which Sherlockian scholars seek to identify a genuine text. The voice of Holmes is not the voice of Watson, and while a case related by Holmes himself is not unique ("The Adventure of the Lion's Mane" comes readily to mind as another example), it does entail stylistic differences which can only serve to perplex those wishing to make a definitive authentication.

It is equally difficult to rule out Watson's contribution entirely. As I have noted, the manuscript is in his own hand and therefore there can be no way of knowing to what degree the doctor altered, shortened, or otherwise amended Holmes's story. Why it was never typed (which would doubtless have entailed more corrections and alterations on Watson's part), I cannot guess.† Holmes may have been off and running onto something else before Watson (who seems to have been asking the questions) had a chance to tidy up a bunch of loose ends. The manuscript does break off with the sudden arrival of Herbert Asquith, and Watson may idly have supposed he could finish it up later—only later never came.

(For that matter, it is impossible to say to what degree Holmes typically exercised editorial control over a Watsonian text. On the

---

*The paper and ink have been vouched for by the forensics department of Scotland Yard and Professor Van Meegrin of the National Gallery, London. The handwriting has been certified as Watson's by two experts in the field whom I am not at liberty to name from Langley, Virginia.

†Perhaps a revised and completed typescript does—or did—exist somewhere else. If it hasn't been destroyed, many of these questions may be answered more fully someday.

one hand, he is constantly quoted as denigrating Watson's efforts, deriding them for their sensational content and their exclusion of pure logic—"produce[ing] much the same effect as if you had worked a love-story or an elopement into the fifth proposition of Euclid"—but on the other hand, it is clear that these same accounts have been published with his consent. Holmes, like many a famous figure, may well have connived at his own public image.)

As for the writing itself, the evidence is contradictory as to whether or not Watson was taking pure dictation. Parts of the manuscript bear the impress of hasty composition; the writing is nearly illegible, with abbreviations and other symptoms of an ad hoc nature, suggesting a kind of improvised shorthand that might have been prompted by the need to keep pace with a speaker. In other places, however, the penmanship, as well as the prose style itself, suggest a more leisurely method of composition, one in which Watson might well be "creating" as opposed to merely copying.

A word about "Americanisms." As I felt obliged to point out in my introduction to the manuscript known as *The West End Horror,* many amateur sleuths believe they can detect a spurious Watson text by pointing out American expressions, thereby concluding that these are forgeries from the New World. It must be reiterated that since both Holmes and Watson spent significant amounts of time in the United States, such "Americanisms" may prove nothing of the kind. Watson practiced medicine in San Francisco (per William Baring-Gould); Holmes spent a good portion of his life in America, both as a young and as an older man. Indeed, at the end of the present manuscript he was bound for Chicago on a case which would consume the better part of two years undercover. He was fond of American English, and by 1914 he was telling Watson that after two years in America, ". . . my well of [English] English seems to be permanently defiled" ("His Last Bow"). As it happens,

American locutions pepper all the Watson case histories, and the novice is advised not to set too much store by them.

Then there is the matter of the title. I don't think I am giving anything away when I note that the canary trainer referred to here proves not to be "Wilson, the notorious canary-trainer" whose death removed a plague spot from the East End of London ("The Adventure of Black Peter"), but someone else entirely. In the title and the chapter headings I detect Watson's own sensibility, though from the text it would appear that Holmes himself referred to a canary trainer more than once, perhaps inspiring Watson with his title.

In sum, I anticipate endless debates in the matter of authenticity but offer no opinions of my own, save this: Holmes in Paris seems at least as likely as Holmes in Tibet, which—as Watson reveals in his text—was questioned by attentive readers as early as 1912! One can only hope that if the manuscript *is* authentic, somehow, some way, in the years to come, scholars and indeed the world at large may be treated to the full story of the so-called missing years, known as the Great Hiatus. (I, for one, was tantalized by the hint Holmes gives Watson at the end of the manuscript as to his next destination.)

I have added the usual explanatory footnotes and corrected Watson's somewhat shaky spelling. There were instances in his scrawl when it was impossible to determine what word or phrase was being employed. In these situations I have done my best to "fill in" what seemed to me the appropriate lines. I have not bracketed these interpolations for fear of disrupting the narrative flow. Nevertheless, if the style that results is occasionally jarring, the fault must rest with me, not Watson.

One final note, so to speak: Holmes's narrative revolves a good deal around classical music, a subject with which I am only glancingly acquainted. In my annotations, therefore, I am not always

equipped to make educated evaluations of Holmes's statements and judgments in this area, for which I hope readers will pardon me.

There is not much else to report. I urge people to write to the folks at Yale and tell them to get their act together.

NICHOLAS MEYER
London, 1993

THE CANARY TRAINER

INTRODUCTORY:
THE DEAD QUEEN

"It is certainly a most mysterious business, Watson. What do you make of it?"

I confess I had heard words not too dissimilar from these on more than one occasion. Yet now, as in the past, I was obliged to own my helplessness.

"The queen is certainly dead," I began. Sherlock Holmes pulled forth a large magnifying glass and peered through it at the corpse.

"Brilliant, Watson. Your capacity for observing the obvious has not deserted you. The queen is most certainly dead. The question is who killed her."

Suppressing my annoyance at a condescension in his tone to which familiarity had failed to inure me, I joined him in contemplation of the body.

She lay quite motionless, defying us to divine the secret of her sudden demise.

"Whom do you suspect?"

"It is a mistake to theorize in advance of data," he reminded me. "Invariably it biases the judgment."

"Do you propose performing an autopsy?"

"That would be difficult," he acknowledged with a thin smile, "though not necessarily impossible."

"I see no marks of violence upon the body," I offered.

"None whatever," the detective concurred, "yet I could swear this was no natural death. Why, only yesterday, she was happily laying eggs, and now she is still as the grave, her crown ready to encircle the brows of another before chaos engulfs her kingdom."

The year was 1912 and the place Burley Manor Farm* on the northern slopes of the Sussex Downs, not quite five miles from Eastbourne, where Holmes and Mrs. Hudson, who had presided over our Baker Street lodgings, were now living in modest retirement. During this time I had occasionally spent a weekend in their company, for in truth their spectacular view of the Channel was less than an hour from my doorstep by the express.

Holmes's retirement was as mysterious to me as everything else about him, as arbitrary, as typical, one might say, of his mercurial temperament. It was almost as if he had risen one morning and decided he was tired of London, for he informed me in the next breath of his intention of moving to the South Downs and raising bees. This was an interest he had seemingly developed out of some researches to which I was not privy.

" 'When a man is tired of London, he is tired of life,' " I re-

---

*The editor has located a Birling Manor Farm in the vicinity described, but not a Burley.

minded him of Johnson's maxim, but his logical mind quickly perceived that this was not a bona fide argument.

"I am not tired of life, I am tired of a life of crime—and of soot," he added, eyeing the dreary rooftops outside our rooms with a sour countenance. "I shall retire and keep bees."

I did my best to discourage this improbable intention, and indeed his early experiments appeared to justify my worst fears. He was stung badly and more than once when I came down to help him get fixed up. It was fortunate that a doctor, namely myself, was near to hand, and more fortunate still that Holmes was not allergic, as some people are, to the venom of bee stings.

Yet he persisted and consulted frequently with his zoological authority, Mr. Sherman, formerly of Lambeth, now himself living in retirement in East Acton. What Sherman didn't know about beekeeping he made it his business to discover on Holmes's behalf. On more than one occasion he journeyed to the detective's country digs and there helped my friend pursue his mania. They spent hours in close consultation outdoors, covered by netting and pointing to this and that in Holmes's arrangements. Their pottering in the garden led to the construction of a series of sheds, knocked up ad lib, which did little, in my view, to improve the appearance of the property.

As Holmes's medical man my reluctance to see him preoccupied by a manifestly dangerous activity was only equalled by my personal perplexity as to its appeal.

"I cannot make out what it is that absorbs you in these buzzing pests," I rebuked him as I treated him one morning for a series of stings which had occurred during one of my early visits. He laughed, winced at my application of alcohol, and lit a cigarette. "Sometimes a complete change is stimulating," he observed. "You are doubtless aware that after writing *War and Peace* Tolstoy took up the study of ancient Greek."

"Ancient Greek would make more sense to me than bees," I countered stubbornly. He sighed.

"I put it to you that bees are an idealized microcosm of humanity," he remarked, blowing smoke with a jerky motion of his head. "Here are your workers, your drones, there your captains of industry, your princes of commerce, yonder your architects and planners, and finally the queen herself, presiding over all, truly the mother of her country. Small wonder the hardworking Mormons chose bees as their device," he added.*

"That strikes me as rather fanciful," I rejoined.

"How so?"

"Well, for one thing, as you must have surely recognized, your society has no criminal element."

"I did say an *idealized* microcosm, my boy."

"But surely, since you regularly lamented the dearth of criminal ingenuity when you maintained your practice as a consulting detective, you cannot now maintain that the contemplation of a society free from that element which was your own greatest source of stimulation can satisfy you?"

"That is a point which had indeed escaped my notice," Holmes rejoined, smiling and sitting up, "and yet I think we may have a thing or two to learn from utopias."

And there the conversation ended, as it so often did, with my winning the battle but losing the war.

As time passed, I must own that Holmes's bees thrived. He was stung less often and finally not at all. His dexterity with smoke and netting increased, as did the bees' trust. After a while it was no longer necessary for Sherman to be involved with Holmes's questions either in person or by telegram. Eventually Holmes surren-

---

*Holmes had certainly become familiar with Mormons through his exposure to them as recounted in *A Study in Scarlet*.

dered the netting itself and wandered freely amongst his hives, a welcome, if not honored, guest.

My own skepticism and puzzlement changed considerably, I must report, when, on a subsequent call in late 1910, I first sampled the honey Holmes managed to extract from the hive. This was so deliciously sweet and went so well with crumpets or with scones that even Mrs. Hudson withdrew her objections to Holmes's eccentric hobby.

"You know, sir," she said to him that Sunday at breakfast, "you could make a handsome living if we was to sell this stuff."

I had the idea she had waited for a visit of mine before raising the subject, as though she might profitably enlist my aid in her scheme.

"Do you really think so, Mrs. Hudson?" Holmes had paused in the act of spreading some honey over a slice of buttered toast.

"There's no doubt of it, sir. We could have our own labels printed and Bill could take the jars to London—or wherever you wanted to set up shop," she amended, seeing Holmes begin to chuckle silently at her project. "Well, it was just an idea," she concluded in an injured tone.

"Mrs. Hudson, you must forgive me. Your notion is a capital one and I shall give it every consideration."

"My principal objection," he confided to me after she had cleared the breakfast things, "is that I settled here with the intention of retiring. I should like to continue my little researches, perhaps do a bit of writing on beekeeping, but I have no intention of going into trade.* Sherlock Holmes's Special Honey sounds like an undertaking that would consume a great deal of the leisure I came here to indulge."

*Holmes's work with bees eventually resulted in the privately printed classic *Practical Handbook of Bee Culture with Some Observations on the Segregation of the Queen* (1914).

As time went by, my weekend visits grew less frequent. Even though the distance between us was comparatively short, my practice and domestic life took up a sufficiency of my time.*

I knew that Holmes sometimes got up to town, but I never saw him on these occasions. The great detective was lured from his retreat when the police of our dizzying metropolis had need of his services. Holmes never objected too strenuously to these occasional calls upon his expertise. He liked to keep his hand in, as he put it, as though to prove to himself that his faculties were still on their mettle.

He made three journeys to London of which I am aware. One concerned the business of the purloined tiger; a second was in connection with the affair of the pied piper; and the circumstances of the last I am not at liberty to divulge. It may be that one day I shall set down the details of these cases, at least one of which would rock the crowned heads of an ancient European dynasty.†

It was June of 1912 before I could be induced to spend three weeks with my old friend, basking in indolence and bees.

In the case of the dead queen, whose demise we now contemplated, Holmes finally deduced that she had been carried off by a late frost. A number of drones had succumbed at the same time, and it was Holmes's conclusion that a freak overnight drop in the temperature was responsible. He had become so knowledgeable by this time that I was disinclined to doubt him.

"And not just about bees, sir," Mrs. Hudson informed me quietly one morning in the kitchen.

"What do you mean?"

---

*There is little record of Watson's life at this period. Evidently he had married again, but the location of his practice remains unclear.

†These journeys to London have not been documented elsewhere. Holmes has left the impression that he remained on the Downs throughout this period.

"I mean the Foreign Secretary's been to see us just before you came down," she informed me in a confidential undertone. "And it weren't about no bees, neither." She shrugged. "But the master sent him packing. Sir Edward weren't a happy man as he left for the station."*

This was a matter I knew better than to pursue.

The days passed agreeably, and I was surprised at how easy it was to fill them. Holmes continued to take all the daily papers and took to scanning them from cover to cover instead of his former practice, which was limited to reading the agony columns and scouring the text for news of sensational or lurid crimes.

"I see they are still hounding Dr. Freud," he remarked one morning, apropos of something on the third page. It is not generally known that Holmes was familiar with the controversial Viennese doctor, but I am forbidden to detail the circumstances of their acquaintance.†

"They still find fault with his theories," I agreed, having also read the piece, which concerned Freud's recent lectures in America.‡

"And from his theories they proceed to misconstrue and ultimately to condemn the man." Holmes shook his head sadly and reached for his new cherrywood. "They entirely miss the point."

"What point is that?"

"Simply this. Dr. Freud is an important, nay a remarkable, figure, regardless of any theory he may have propounded. It boots

---

*The Foreign Secretary at the time was Sir Edward Grey.

†The full details of Holmes's relations with Sigmund Freud was not set down by Watson until 1939. The so-called Swingline-Dobson text (named for the stenographer who transcribed the aged Watson's oral history of the affair) was not discovered for over thirty years and was published in 1974 under the title *The Seven-Per-Cent Solution*.

‡Watson's memory or record-keeping plays him false. Or else he was employing writer's license: Freud visited America in 1909.

not whether his theories are correct, whether his suppositions about women, children, or even dreams are accurate. It does not matter whether he is a man of upstanding character or a villain. None of these things has anything to do with his claim to immortality.''

"You feel he has such a claim?"

"Without doubt."

"Upon what is it based?"

"Cartography." I know my jaw must have dropped, so great was my astonishment at this unexpected retort.

"I never knew Freud to draw maps."

"I assure you he has, though they may not be entirely reliable."

"Holmes, you mystify me. How can a map be of any value if it is inaccurate?"

"On the contrary," he paused, lighting his pipe and puffing vigorously to get it going, "the fact that Freud's maps may be in error does not invalidate their importance. The proper comparison with Freud is Columbus. Does anyone remember or care that Columbus supposed he had reached India? In this respect Columbus's charts were wildly inaccurate. That seems, in retrospect, less important than the fact that Columbus was the first white man to set foot on a hitherto unexplored continent, the very existence of which was unknown to the vast majority of mankind. Columbus is rightly famous, and nobody troubles to recall that his map was entirely wrong."

"And what is the map Sigmund Freud has drawn? Upon what unexplored continent has he set foot?"

"Upon the continent of the so-called unconscious. He is the first scientist to deduce and then to certify its existence. If his maps of that *terra incognita* are a bit hazy, you must excuse my failure to become particularly incensed. Compared to his actual discovery, you will readily perceive their insignificance."

With these and a score of like examples, Holmes proved that though he might have been living in what he chose to call retirement, yet his faculties remained as keen as ever. It was in the second week of my holiday that he provided me with another of those little glimpses of his intelligence which never failed to astonish and delight.

"You are right, Watson, it is indeed inconceivable," he stated one evening, out of the blue, as I sat gazing into the fire.

"What is inconceivable?"

"The sinking of the *Titanic.* You needn't look so astonished, my dear fellow. I see that you have been staring in puzzlement at the Cunarder over the mantel. Then you took your eyes from the ship and reread your *Times,* which doubtless contains more speculation regarding the tragedy. Then you sighed and permitted yourself to be mesmerized by the fire. It was no great matter to infer your melancholy thoughts."

I confessed he had inferred them correctly. It *was* inconceivable to me that such a thing could happen.

"It was certainly a very long shot," Holmes concurred. "The unhappy architect could hardly have envisioned the consequences of his design."

"What are you getting at?"

"A most unlikely chain of events, Watson. The hull of the *Titanic,* as is well known, was divided into watertight compartments."

"The papers have stressed the fact."

"Yet these same divisions went no higher than E Deck, which is to say hardly above her waterline. It would appear that for aesthetic considerations, Mr. Andrews was reluctant to continue his watertight-bulkhead scheme. He had no wish to break up his large public rooms."

"What of that?"

"When the unfortunate ship struck the iceberg, she was sliced open along the starboard side of the hull from the bow. Water poured in, pulling her down by the head. As the bow dipped lower into the sea, it was an inevitable process for water to spill *over* the top of the first watertight compartment into the second and so into the next, and so on into the next. She must have sunk almost perpendicular to the ocean.''

''What a ghastly business. I say, how did you know about the watertight compartments going only so high as E-deck?''

''I assure you it is in the paper, my dear fellow. Most data are, if you are patient and thorough enough to root for them like a pig in search of truffles. The rest is merely a series of reasonable inferences. Unprovable, of course, in this case, since the unhappy vessel is now and forever beyond the reach of men.''

In the tranquillity that characterized my visit, I spent a goodly portion of my time in the extensive reorganization and revision of the copious notes I had made of various cases in which it had been my good fortune to assist my companion over the course of a distinguished career. Some of these cases, it is true, could hardly be termed sensational. They chiefly turned on elements small and indeed domestic; some had no real criminal activity to them at all, yet they presented what Holmes liked to refer to as ''features of interest,'' touches either bizarre or *outré,* that warranted inclusion in my annals. Other cases, by contrast, were of such a sensational nature that I was frequently obliged to alter names and sometimes even critical details in order to present them safely before the public. I have borne a good many taunts and insults regarding my intelligence as the result of some of my balder fabrications, which changes I would never have promulgated but for the insistence of my principal.*

*Watson has been twitted for not remembering where he was wounded at the battle of Maiwand (leg or shoulder?) and what his landlady's name was

Holmes, I have noted elsewhere, was vain as any girl where his gifts were concerned, and yet at the same time was bound by the need for discretion which must be one of the tools of the trade for anyone engaged in work like his. (He was no longer, it must be said, the world's only consulting detective.)

My place in his universe was most agreeable to him. If Holmes was the sun at the center of his own cosmos, I orbited him like a friendly satellite, basking in reflected light. I set down details of his cases when I had his permission to do so, and while he was free to criticize my efforts and commented with a sneer upon what he called my penchant for the melodramatic, yet I knew how secretly pleased he was by the attention the publication of my works brought him. When at last I had his leave to publish my account of his triumph in Dartmoor, the presses could hardly keep pace with the demand. Some said the Hound represented Holmes's finest hour.

I knew, however, that there were other hours—many of them of which the public had not the slightest inkling—and one of the motives behind my three-week hiatus (though he knew it not) was to cajole him into filling some gaps in my chronology.

The trick was to ferret out missing cases and wheedle Holmes into letting me publish them. He was fond of secrets, was Holmes, and kept snugged away in his storehouse of a memory many tantalizingly obscure references and peculiar histories. I can remember, for example, an astonishing seven years' passage of time in our relations during which he entirely concealed from me the existence of his brother Mycroft. When this revelation was at last made manifest, it was in the most offhand manner imaginable. I recall my further stupefaction at learning that his brother lived at the Dioge-

---

(Mrs. Hudson, Mrs. Turner?), and for a thousand other seeming bloopers of one kind or another.

nes Club in Pall Mall, a mere twenty minutes away from our lodgings in the same city.

"Ah, but not in the same world," Holmes had chuckled when I pointed this out to him.

I would never have heard the whole story of the canary trainer had I not attempted one afternoon to pin him down on the details of his travels following the death of his nemesis, Professor Moriarty.

The days were hot and agreeably long; Holmes's apian endeavors were crowned with success, as the incessant buzzing about our premises proclaimed. He was happily occupied in the extraction of another sweet harvest when I made so bold as to call on him.

"Hullo, Watson, what brings you to my place of business?" he wondered cheerfully. "Take care you move slowly, my dear chap. They don't know your scent."

"I would greatly appreciate it, then, if you would call upon me at *my* place of business at your earliest convenience," I told him, glancing apprehensively about me. "My study," I explained, seeing that he did not entirely grasp my meaning.

"Give me just five minutes to tidy myself up, there's a good fellow."

Twenty minutes later I had settled him in a chair opposite the banged-up deal table I had appropriated for my own use and given him a cup of tea, into which he was stirring large amounts of his new specialty.

"Now then, Watson, what has brought you into my hive?"

"Curiosity."

"About my bees?" I saw his face brighten at the prospect of answering my questions and sharing his passion with me at last.

"About your dates." His face fell at this, and he stretched his gaunt frame with a grimace. "Holmes, I really must insist. There are irregularities here that have made me a laughingstock. Take, for example, 1891 to 1894."

He smiled and rolled his eyes.

"The so-called Lost Years."

"When you left Professor—"

"Moriarty," he interposed forcefully.*

"Very well, when you left Professor Moriarty. You have favored me with the most improbable account of your activities during the interregnum preceding your return to London."

"My dear fellow, if you persist in spelling 'Lama' with two *l*'s, it is hardly astonishing that your readers wonder if I haven't been to Peru instead of Tibet. My claim to have met with the High Lama appears absurd if you give that august personage the spelling of a South American mammal. The same difficulty arises," he went on, warming to his thesis before I could object, "when you spell Montpellier with one *l*—you and your *l*'s, my dear Watson!—and try to convince your readers I was in France and not the capital of Vermont."

"All of which is entirely diversionary," I protested. "There was a civil war raging when you claim to have seen the Caliph at Khartoum. Really, I think I have a right to know the truth. What sort of biographer is it that knowingly perpetuates such distortions?"

"You raise a very knotty problem, if I may say so," he answered, his eyes twinkling. "Someone did say that a biography ought to be written by an enemy."

"You still have not addressed my question. What really occupied you during those years?"

He stared at me for some moments, pressing the tips of his fingers together as was his habit when listening or thinking. I feared to interrupt him while he considered my request, knowing that a

---

*Clearly Holmes is here emphasizing his agreement with Watson to maintain the fiction of the death duel at the Reichenbach falls. The truth behind this fiction was not to be made public until after Freud's death, a stipulation Watson scrupulously honored. (See *The Seven-Per-Cent Solution*.)

single untoward remark might cause him to close up like a clam. I therefore held my breath, hoping for that which I had long sought to learn.

"It can scarcely be of interest to you," he said at last.

"Now you are fishing. You know very well that I regard it as of crucial importance."

He paused again and stroked a corner of his mouth with an index finger. He was not above playing the coquette in matters of this sort. For my part, I attempted a look of indifference as I waited for the vagaries of his mood to manifest themselves in one direction or the other.

"It was certainly rather more involved than I let on," he said grudgingly and reached for his tea. "You are talking about three years," he added, as if to say, You cannot possibly expect me to sit here and recount three whole years' worth of incident.

"If you would only give me some rough idea of what really did happen," I offered, "or tell me anything of particular interest. It need not be made public until such time as you see fit." I threw this last in with the notion of coaxing him as I had sometimes done in the past.

"Kindly do not patronize me, Doctor," said he. "I am well aware of your little tricks."

Nevertheless he had begun to fill his pipe with shag, and I felt the tension ease between my shoulders. Cigarettes were for conversation; the pipe was a sure sign of a narrative to come. I had seen the relation between the two often enough to comprehend their portent.

"I will tell you one part of my journey," he offered finally, like Scheherazade. "It may be that at some future date you may tempt me into relating others."

"I am all attention," said I, laying out my pen and papers.

"It was a curious business," he went on, casting his eyes to the

ceiling as though he had forgot me already, "some of it high comedy, no doubt; other parts so tragic as to please Aristotle. I allowed myself to be blackmailed and made several serious blunders besides. Altogether an unforgivable performance in one of the most singular cases in which I was ever called upon to act."

"I had no idea you undertook any cases during this period."

"I would not have volunteered for this one for worlds," he commented with a bleak expression, closing his eyes. "You have heard me say that a doctor gone wrong is the first of criminals,* my dear fellow, but I assure you he is as nothing compared to a madman."

"You intrigue me."

He opened his eyes and favored me with a winning smile.

"As I intended, my dear Watson."

*This appears to refer to an observation made by Holmes in the case Watson titled "One Adventure of the Speckled Band."

1

RETURNED TO LIFE

One of the first things that struck me after Reichenbach, Watson, was that no one dreamt I was alive.* Thanks to the account you were likely to write, my dear fellow, there was every reason for the world to suppose me dead, and this, I suddenly understood, provided me with a heaven-sent opportunity afforded few of us in this life, that of starting afresh.

How delicious a prospect, the more so because it was so un-

---

*Holmes or Watson here as elsewhere is playing fast and loose with the details of Holmes's mental collapse. Believing that the truth would never be told, the present manuscript, written years in advance of *The Seven-Per-Cent Solution,* attempts to hew to the "official" version of events—i.e., Professor Moriarty and the death duel at the Reichenbach falls in Switzerland—but is unable to suppress certain other essential details such as oblique allusions to Holmes's doctor, Sigmund Freud, or the name Sigerson, which Holmes told Watson would be his *nom de guerre* as a travelling violinist, following his departure from therapy in Vienna.

looked for! I had been arbitrarily thrust into a unique position, and as I considered its bewildering implications, I became positively giddy, overcome by an almost childish hilarity at the avenues newly open to me.

I had certainly been through a period of enormous personal difficulty, and it seemed utterly appropriate that I treat myself to some little holiday, allow myself to wander where I liked, basking in the (to me) heady joys of anonymity. For while it is true that I have enjoyed the plaudits of the multitude, thanks to your lively if inaccurate accounts, my dear Watson, it is also true that notoriety over time can be a kind of curse, weighing upon the shoulders of him that staggers beneath it. Perhaps I had not even noticed the degree to which I stooped under its yoke until I was abruptly confronted by the possibility of dispensing with it altogether.

Travelling under the name Sigerson, as you know, I boarded the train for Milan with no particular end in view save that of getting away, journeying to some locale with which I was unfamiliar and stimulating myself with strange sights and different sounds. I judged that with time these irresponsible longings would diminish and I should again devote myself to that work for which I was intended, but if I had learnt anything from a certain doctor, it was not to subject myself exclusively to a regimen which threatened my mental equanimity.

Milan, I confess, did not agree with me. I found myself in a smoky, unattractive industrial city and, after touring the Duomo, decided not to remain there long.

With more time to consider the matter, it now occurred to me that the place I should really like to visit was Paris, a city I scarcely knew, which was ironic, as I am of French descent.* I had been

---

*Holmes traced his line of ancestry to the sister of the French artist Émile Jean Horace Vernet (1789–1863).

there as a young man, but always briefly and always passing through on my way to some other terminus. Over the years, as you are aware, I had preferred to remain in London, knowing the unhealthy excitement engendered in the criminal classes when they learnt I was from town. In the euphoria of my newfound second life, however, these considerations mattered not a whit, paled in fact, beside the sudden realization that I could go to Paris if I so wished, and explore that city, which has been called the capital of the nineteenth century.

It was a simple matter to book myself aboard another train, and fifty-two hours after the caprice had popped into my brain, Mr. Henrik Sigerson of Oslo found himself wandering the streets of the most beautiful metropolis in the world.

Now as it happens I am one of those curious people who cannot feel at ease in new surroundings unless they find out first everything they can about them. I need, in short, to know how things came to be before I can organize my mind to make sense of how they are.

Before leaving the Gare d'Orsay, therefore, I purchased a Baedeker and other like material and sat on a bench across from the river facing the Jardin des Tuilleries, eating a sandwich and learning about the place in which I now found myself.

Paris, it appeared, took its name from an ancient Gallic tribe, the Parisii, who were settled upon this marshy area when they were subdued by the legions of Julius Caesar. The Romans called the place Lutecia, and like London, Paris began civilized life as a Roman camp. It started on the Ile Saint-Louis and the Ile de la Cité in the middle of the river Seine, but soon overflowed the river's banks on either side, evolving over the years, higgledy-piggledy fashion, into a labyrinthine warren of mean little streets and uninviting alleys. The kings of France were so disgusted by the place that they chose to live outside it and constructed Versailles for the purpose.

This was certainly not the Paris which confronted me as I nibbled my sandwich, and, reading on, I was mildly astonished to learn that the transformation of this medieval hodgepodge into the world-renowned City of Light was only accomplished within the last forty years! I see you smile, Watson. Doubtless you are staggered by my ignorance, but as I have told you more than once, the mind is an attic with limited storage, and I had previously reserved the space at my disposal for facts which bore upon my art. I recall how astonished you were when I told you that I had no idea whether the earth revolved about the sun or the sun about the earth, as it made no difference to my work.*

The transformation of Paris, I now learned, was the work of the Emperor Louis Napoleon, who styled himself Napoleon III, the nephew of the Little Corporal, but who, as I should judge, was no more his nephew than I am, but rather a rogue, who combined cunning and effrontery in equal measure when he seized power and proclaimed himself the monarch of a putative second empire.

This Napoleon, who had all the legitimacy of a comic operetta pirate king, told his architect, one Baron Haussmann, that Paris needed "opening up" if it was to compare with the rest of the world as a modern European capital worthy of the name.

The Emperor's true reasons appeared to have been rather more pragmatic. In its long history, Paris had had its share of revolutions and insurrections, and every time they occurred was heard the same cry, *"Aux barricades!"* Since the streets were so many and narrow it was a simple matter for the rebellious populace to seal them off with furniture and wagons, compelling the forces of incumbency to take them one by one, indeed, house by house.

*For this and other examples of Holmes's shocking ignorance, see *A Study in Scarlet.*

Whether Haussmann knew or cared what Louis Napoleon's real motives were in the matter I was unable to learn from Thomas Cook, but he discharged his mission with messianic zeal. He procured a map of the city and, beginning at the Arc de Triomphe, drew a series of twelve lines, rather like the spokes of a wheel or the radii of a star. Each of these lines became a broad boulevard, so wide that no one would ever again be able to seal off the streets of the city from the authority of the ruling order. During the spurious Emperor's reign, Paris saw a building program unequalled in the history of any metropolis. The city must have quaked under the din, choked on its own dust, and I cannot imagine what became of the dispossessed multitudes who saw their hovels leveled by Napoleon's architect, the man who became known to all and sundry as "the Surgeon."

I had myself procured a map at the station, and, my snack concluded, I began a circumambulation of the city, astounded at the magnificent thoroughfares created by the cynical tyrant.

Contrasted with London, Paris is a small city, and in a matter of days I was able to acquaint myself with a certain portion of its anatomy, delighting in its uniformity of pinkish slate stone, its grey roofs of the type called mansard, and its blue-and-gold skies. Twilight, which Parisians call *l'heure bleu,* the blue hour, has no equivalent anywhere else that I know of.

I began by crossing the river and walking to the Champs Élysées, a promenade I am confident has no rival on this earth. At one end I perceived the first Napoleon's enormous triumphal arch, but rather than trudge uphill towards it for what I estimated was the better part of a mile, I allowed gravity to direct my steps and strolled in the opposite direction to the Place de la Concorde, formerly the Place de la Révolution, the very spot on which the guillotine stood and performed its horrendous labor, chopping off the heads of almost fifteen hundred victims. Instead of rivers of blood, the vast square was now choking on horses and carriages of all descriptions.

I cannot remember all of the sites I visited that first day, but I do recall that every other shop was a restaurant or brasserie and that whenever I grew tired or hungry, there was always a sidewalk café in which to rest one's weary limbs and the food to be found there was uniformly sinful. You will be interested (and perhaps amused) to learn that my sojourn in Paris was the only time in my adult life when I put on weight!

It goes without saying—and therefore I shall not dwell on the fact—that no visit to modern Paris is complete without making an ascent of Monsieur Eiffel's curious tower. Let it merely be noted that I proved no exception to this rule.

Eventually, I stopped at an hotel on the *rive gauche,* opposite Notre Dame, in the Rue Saint-Julien-le-Pauvre. Called the Esmeralda, it was fittingly named for the heroine of Hugo's remarkable novel, who must (presumably) have lived nearby. The building itself dated from the fifteenth century, and the rooms were tiny but they would do until I found something better.

Yes, I had decided to stay in Paris for a time. The city was irresistible, and in my present emancipated humor I determined to explore it. There was a final incentive, I own, to this decision, and that was my chance discovery of a *Daily Telegraph* in which my death was reported in some detail. This number came to hand in one of those countless cafés to which I have alluded, left there, doubtless, by some traveller with no further use for it.

I sat sipping my *café au lait* and smoking a morning cigarette whilst I took in the eerie confirmation of my demise. Watson, you were reliable as always. Indeed, it was hard to remain unmoved as I read of my death struggle with Moriarty—poor old Moriarty!— and of the grief it instilled in thousands of mourners. Former clients of mine were interviewed (including a certain gracious lady

who resides in Windsor), all of whose sorrow was almost sufficient to bring tears to my eyes.*

But not quite. I had by no means got over the discovery of my newfound liberty, and I am afraid the novelty of my situation had not yet begun to wear off. (Years later, when I finally got round to reading the novel, I understood with a shock of recognition the feelings of Tom Sawyer while attending his own funeral.) Subsequent articles on the subject of my death in *Le Monde* and *Le Figaro*—"*Sherlock Holmes Mort!*" et cetera,—with interesting embellishments typical of French journalism—likewise failed to sway me. Rather they served only to strengthen my resolve, reemphasizing my unlikely emancipation and its novel rewards.

I should interrupt myself long enough to state that my newfound deliverance from the shackles of my former self did not tempt me to the careless resumption of any old habits. You needn't feign ignorance, my dear fellow; I refer to my past penchant for certain narcotics when no cases of sufficient interest presented themselves to intrigue me. That part of my life was truly over; thanks to our friend, I had put away childish things, and in the whole sorry account which follows I was only tempted to have recourse to them once, as you shall hear.

Soon after the chance encounter with my own obituary, I found lodgings in the Marias district in the Rue Saint-Antoine. My apartments were quite Spartan compared with our Baker Street digs—a mere two rooms in number and four flights up—presided over by an octogenarian concierge, Madame Solange, who brought me fresh croissants and hot chocolate each morning, grumbling incessantly the while. But what were rooms to me, who needed only a place to rest my head at night? It was a simple matter to unpack my Gladstone and take stock of my circumstances.

---

*I have been unable to track down this issue of the *Telegraph*.

Now that I was well and truly ensconced, I was faced with the question of what it was I planned to do. I knew no one in the city, but as I have never been what is called a sociable creature, this did not trouble me in the least. There was only one friend worthy of the name I had ever known (your blushes, Watson!), and in his absence I was happily indifferent to the prospect of any others.

I realized that I had no need for work as such. I could always wire Mycroft for a draft, but that was scarcely the point.* I could not simply pass the days wandering about the city without any purpose. A tourist can never learn anything but superficialities with that pro-gramme. I needed a *raison d'être.*

I toyed briefly with the notion of setting up as a detective, but surrendered the idea almost at once as impracticable. While my French was excellent, there seemed little point in merely resuming the vocation which I had so recently abandoned and with which I was at present so disenchanted. I had no real knowledge of the city and its inhabitants; in functioning as a detective in such circum-stances I would be impossibly hobbled. Worse, should I succeed in hanging out my shingle, it would only be a matter of time before my presence became sufficiently conspicuous as to undo my incognito.

You will recall that I was travelling with a violin. I began by kitting myself out as a violin instructor, tacking up solicitations on notice boards and soon gaining a small clientele, mostly children, but including one retired infantryman named Guzot who, having survived the Franco-Prussian War and the Commune, now pro-posed to enjoy the autumn of his life by learning to fiddle.

My teaching income enabled me to live without contacting Mycroft, but it did try my patience and strain relations with my neighbors. Students of the piano may make mistakes, but pianists

*Holmes's brother knew that he had not perished, as did his house-keeper, Mrs. Hudson.

do not make their own notes, they are merely obliged to strike them correctly. Violinists, on the other hand, must create the notes they play, and these can be excruciating, especially when produced by novices.

My pupils, I fear, were no exception. I had a promising eight-year-old, but the rest, including dear old Guzot, invariably left me with a headache. Madame Solange herself was not so deaf nor so distant in her ground-floor quarters that she did not complain and threaten to evict me.

"Monsieur Sigerson, you go too far!" she exclaimed. "Who can endure these vile sounds? To *you* I am willing to listen," she went on, alluding to my regular practice. "To *them,* I am not!"

I had to admit she had a point, and rather than trespass further on her fragile sensibilities, I cast about for some other means of livelihood.

It was while pondering this question that I was overtaken by a series of events which combined to resolve the issue while at the same time plunging me into the singular business I now propose to relate.

I determined to attend a performance of *Le Prophète* at the Paris Opéra, known familiarly after its architect as the Palais Garnier. You know my great fondness for opera as a musical form, Watson, though I am aware you do not share my taste. Opera seems to me to combine the elements of drama with the unique capacity for the simultaneous expression of interior thought and emotion. *Le Prophète* of Meyerbeer was not exactly my cup of tea, but it happened to be on. With the thought of distracting myself from the collapse of my career as a violin instructor, I hailed a cab and set forth.

Even the grandiose excesses of the Second Empire had not prepared me for my first sight of the Palais Garnier. The Emperor, as I judged, was never a man to miss the opportunity to impress.

Haussmann, his creature, did not seek to create merely an opera house, but rather an enormous intersection where no less than seven of his spectacular boulevards converged, one of them, fittingly, named for himself. At the end of each of these enormous avenues other monuments contrive to overwhelm the eye—the Madeleine, the Place Vendôme, the Place de la Concorde—but the central feature, the fixed hub of all this gargantuan symmetry, is the great opera house itself, which was to play so conspicuous a part in my life.

Looking at it, that first September evening,* lit from within and glittering like a multifaceted jewel without, I was unable to gauge its true size and complexity. These were to become more apparent in the days and weeks which followed.

If you have ever entered the main foyer of the Paris Opéra you will know that no powers of description can do justice to the Byzantine opulence of the place. The grand staircase alone, with its line of human statuary, the Garde Républicaine, with swords, white breeches, shining black boots, and gleaming horsehair-plumed helmets, seems to have been designed to overawe the visitor whilst at the same time making him feel part of larger-than-life events taking place here—which in reality consist of nothing more remarkable than going up or down a set of stairs.

Inside the theatre, a stupendous chandelier was suspended above an audience of some two thousand lavishly appointed guests whose collective glitter was eclipsed only by the spectacle onstage. The Palais Garnier boasts the largest proscenium in the world, and the night I attended at least five hundred supernumeraries, to say nothing of six or seven horses, crowded the platform in a presenta-

---

*September adds some confusion to this history. According to Watson, the events chronicled under the title *The Seven-Per-Cent Solution* began towards the end of April, 1891. It is doubtful that the entire affair consumed all of five months. Perhaps Holmes stopped in Milan for longer than he admits?

tion of grandeur and detail that was unlike anything I had ever beheld. Real armor, enormous banners, and genuine gold and silver dazzled the eye as sumptuous panoramas succeeded one another throughout the evening. They were so many and so much that it became possible to conceive of a production wherein the onstage population outnumbered the spectators!

At the commencement of the third act, the production outdid itself. To stupefied gasps of admiration mixed with incredulity, the *corps de ballet,* wearing ice skates, performed on *real* ice!

It seems of lesser moment to report that the acoustics of the house were excellent and poor old Meyerbeer was given more than his due from the pit and by the singers, especially the young soprano, Christine Daaé, in the role of Berthe. This young woman sang beautifully and was a beauty herself into the bargain. I was not the only one to gasp in admiration at the purity of her vocal technique, the conviction of her acting, and the sweetness of her appearance. I was able to determine that Daaé was a relatively new addition to the opera's arsenal, and I overheard members of the audience during the interval predicting great things for her.

One thing attracted my notice at the time. The house was sold out, as I was able to satisfy myself, turning and surveying my neighbors during the *entr'acte*—with one curious exception. There was an empty box in the grand tier. How odd, I remember thinking, the more so as I saw folk queuing outside the theatre earlier, clearly hoping to benefit from last-minute cancellations. I dismissed the matter from my mind—no doubt the box belonged to some eccentric personage who kept it on reserve whether he chose to occupy it or no.

Little did I dream how right I was.

Whatever one thinks of Meyerbeer's music, the whole thing went off without a hitch, and it must have been midnight after all five acts, when I emerged from the dream world I had occupied for

over four hours, into the hurly-burly of the Place de l'Opéra and the chilly night air. I was about to wander across to the Café de la Paix nearby for a little light supper when I became aware of a commotion at the backstage door, near the Rue Gluck, where the artistes enter and exit the theatre.

The hubbub drew me closer, and I watched as people attempted to restrain a middle-aged gentleman in evening clothes, who carried a violin case and appeared to be jerking his way desperately through the protesting crowd.

"Never!" he cried, tearing through the press with his violin. "I would rather die than play another performance in this godforsaken place!" He passed quite near to me, and I can only describe his wild-eyed expression as that of a man whose reason hung by a thread.

Despite entreaties and some laughter in his wake, the violinist lurched off into the traffic of the Place de l'Opéra. He was so disoriented that, looking in the wrong direction, he was instantly felled by a carriage. I rushed to retrieve him as a second crowd now collected about him.

"Let me fetch a doctor," I offered, seeing that blood was streaming down his forehead where it had smacked the kerb.

"Let me go, devil take you!" was his only response. He hurled other like expressions at well-meaning people as he forced his way through them. I could only watch as he staggered past me a second time, clutching his fiddle case to him like a life preserver. He soon blended in with the swirling multitude and was lost from view. I had no idea what had thrown the violinist into such a state, but the whole incident had suddenly given me an idea.

"Will you be needing another violinist?" I inquired at the stage door.

"Auditions tomorrow at two-thirty," growled an elderly man

of large girth and few teeth, whose job, it appeared, was to prevent unwanted visitors from crossing the threshold.

"Why did that fellow—?"

"Why? Who knows why anything around here!" he shouted at me. "Do you speak French? *Two-thirty tomorrow!*"

"Two-thirty."

Trying to possess myself in patience, I returned to my flat, where I restrung and retuned my violin. I practiced all the following morning and lunchtime, ceasing only after repeated knocks on my sitting-room wall implied that worse was to come should I not desist. I rehearsed the scherzo from *A Midsummer Night's Dream* and the "Meditation" from *Thaïs,* which I judged should give any listener a fair account of my abilities.

In my mind the question of my livelihood had been abruptly resolved. The only marvel, in retrospect, was that it had taken so long for the light to dawn. Now that the idea had occurred to me, I became consumed with the notion of winning the post, of playing my violin in the pit of the Paris Opéra, of singing (in a manner of speaking) for my supper. I did not for one moment imagine that this was to become my life's work, but in my present humor the whim had become the summit of my ambition.

The next day I used the artistes' entrance (with a thrill, I confess it), and found myself in the company of six or seven other applicants, all of whom glared nervously at one another whilst waiting to be called. My own nervousness increased as I sat there, for I noticed that the violinists who went in before me did not stay long, but came whirling out again very soon, as if propelled by a revolving door of the type lately installed in the better class of hotels and restaurants. Occasionally I could hear a sort of bellow from the room beyond, and once I thought I heard the crack of a flying object coming into contact with the wall behind my head. How I wished I had my cherished Stradivarius instead of the second-rate instrument upon which I would shortly be called upon to perform.*

"Does anyone know why that fellow resigned?" I asked the man sitting next to me.

"Nerves, I expect," he answered in a dry voice.

This answer meant nothing to me, and as no more information on the subject was forthcoming, I kept my own counsel.

At last I was summoned. Discreetly wiping my moist palms on the sides of my trousers, I took my violin and stepped into a kind of greenroom, decorated with mirrors and large, inferior paintings.

It is hard to describe at this time how much and how badly I wished to win that post. I had never auditioned for any position since my early days as an actor, but the thrill of once again being backstage at a theatre—let alone *this* theatre!—ignited an ambition of which I was previously unaware.† It is often so with human nature; we take for granted and disparage our greatest gifts and yearn to be accepted in capacities for which others might be better suited. Clowns long to enact Hamlet, doctors to write novels, and in my case here was a detective determined to play the violin.

The room in which I found myself was enormous beyond my

---

*Worth five hundred guineas, Holmes's London Stradivarius had been purchased in the Tottenham Court Road for only fifty-five shillings (see "The Adventure of the Cardboard Box"). It was subsequently purchased by the Rockefeller Foundation and used exclusively by Jascha Heifetz. Holmes's present instrument had belonged to an uncle of Freud's (see *The Seven-Per-Cent Solution*).

†"In your case, Holmes, what the law has gained the stage has lost," Baron Dowson told Holmes on the eve of his hanging (see "The Adventure of the Mazarin Stone"). In *The West End Horror* we learn that Holmes as a child made his debut with Henry Irving. (See also Baring-Gould's life of Holmes for a chapter on his tour of America as a member of a theatrical company in 1879.)

expectations. Indeed, almost every space at the Paris Opéra had been designed as if for occupancy by giants. Unlike those responsible for the dingy facilities grudged the artistes at Covent Garden, the Emperor's minions had spared no expense in providing for audience and performers alike.

This greenroom (I later learned there are *six!*) was intended by Garnier as part of a series of more or less private apartments set aside for the Emperor's personal diversions. Originally conceived for midnight suppers and special rendezvous, it was used by the current management for auditions and the occasional cast parties. At the moment it was empty save for a music stand and before it a plain deal table and three rickety chairs, presently occupied by a triumvirate of black-suited gentlemen, none of whom deigned to rise when I entered.

The most curious feature of the place was a folded Japanese screen at the far end of the room, towards which my three inquisitors threw anxious glances.

"My name is—" I began.

"No names!" roared a voice from behind the screen. I recognized the stentorian tones I had discerned while awaiting my turn in the outer chamber. "What will you play?" the voice went on. I responded with my proposed programme. I thought one of the inquisitors smiled.

"Not yet. Not yet!" proclaimed the invisible judge. "Let us begin with a C major scale."

I was unable to conceal my surprise.

"Merely a simple scale?"

"You think the C major is so easy?" demanded the voice. "Remember, every note must be hit squarely in the middle and given exactly the same emphasis. You must climb up; you must go back down. There can be no mistakes. Every note must be true."

It is hard to credit, but the rogue had actually succeeded in terrifying me with the proposition of an elementary scale. I now perceived the purpose of the screen which concealed my noisy interlocutor; it was not merely to intimidate applicants, though doubtless it had that effect, but rather to guarantee that each would be judged by his musical abilities alone. My examiner would have no way of knowing anything about me save the sounds produced by my instrument.

This thought had the happy effect of reassuring me, and I played him the scale. There was a long silence at the conclusion, and the faces at the table stared at the screen.

"Again," it commanded finally. I repeated my performance and fancied that I heard humming this time, though somewhat out of tune.

"Now the Mendelssohn." I launched into the scherzo, and the humming grew louder, still off-key. The troika appeared to relax.

"The Massenet."

I played the "Meditation," and before I had finished, a towering figure emerged from his place of concealment. He was a florid-faced individual with a large head, surmounted by wild, curling locks, just beginning to grey at the temples. His lips were quite thick and the lower of the two rather pendulous, as if from being constantly protruded by its owner. He approached me, smiling myopically with dark eyes, as the others stood to attention as if on parade.

"You are not French," he proclaimed, shaking my hand.

"Non, maître."

"I thought not. The French do not produce violinists."

"I am Norwegian," I told him. "My name is Henrik Sigerson."

At this he shot me a narrow look from beneath a pair of bushy brows, then shook his head with a gruff laugh. "I would not have guessed it," was all he said. "I am the musical director of the Paris Opéra, Maître Gaston Leroux."

"Bonjour, maître."

Again he inclined his large head. "I am responsible for everything that happens here. The smallest detail does not escape my attention. I am in complete command."

There was something in his posture as he said this that seemed to include the trio of silent black-suited fellows in this remark. Whatever his purpose, they chose not to dispute his assertion.

"You play well," he conceded, also apparently for their benefit.

"Thank you. *Maître,* would you care to hear some compositions of my own devising?"*

"Certainly not." The idea appeared to amaze him, but he soon recollected himself. "When can you start?"

"Whenever you like."

"Rehearsals for the orchestra take place every morning at ten. Performances are scheduled for eight. You are expected to be in the theatre and *signed* in . . ."—he stressed the word with a sibilant emphasis—"at least one half hour before time. Am I clear on this point?"

"Perfectly."

He grunted and started for the door, then turned.

"You know what was the fate of your predecessor?"

"I have not the least idea."

"This place abounds with rumors. Pay no attention to them."

With that he was gone.

---

*Watson more than once alludes to Holmes's predilection for his own improvisations over the standard violin repertoire.

2

LITTLE THINGS

*L*ooking back on the entire peculiar affair, I find myself wondering why it was I should have been so slow to recognize anything amiss. Part of it, I think it safe to say, was the feeling that like the rest of me, my faculties were on holiday. My eyes and ears were so overwhelmed by new impressions (and those now received from a stage-struck point of view) that I was reluctant to subject them to formal analysis. Instead I chose to surrender to the experience, to drift along on a current of dreamy impressions deliberately at odds with my professional *modus operandi*.

I must own as well that in this place I was deprived of my normal frames of reference. In order to conclude that something is irregular it is helpful if you are familiar with what is regular. France, Paris, the unfamiliarity of the language and even of the vast opera house itself and its workings—all these combined to produce a

disorienting but not disagreeable sensation that served to lull my powers.

And yet the signs were present all the while.

The very next morning, determined to be *à l'heure,* I arrived before Leroux's stipulated thirty minutes, and promptly lost my way in the mazelike substructure of the theatre, endeavoring to find the orchestra pit. The guardian of the artistes' entrance, the almost toothless behemoth whom I now knew to be called Jérôme, directed me with a brusque gesture towards a spiral iron stairway at the lower end of the entry hall.

These steps led up as well as down. Assuming my destination to be below, I soon found myself traversing an endless network of platforms and further stairs, curving corridors, small doorways, walking past enormous props and gigantic sets, and occasionally peeping over vast, yawning patches of blackness, sensing rather than seeing there a cavernous vacuum. I realized later than I could have wished that I was headed in the wrong direction, whereupon I determined to retrace my steps.

Alas, this proved rather more difficult than I should have imagined. The different levels, doorways, passages, and indifferent illumination all contrived to turn me hopelessly around. Impossible to believe, but I was lost.

Somewhere I thought I heard echoing laughter at my plight. I was saved from my mounting confusion by the appearance of an elderly personage of unsteady carriage, whom I encountered at an intersection. He carried a half-empty open bottle of wine, and his flushed complexion suggested that he had partaken of its contents without the intermediate formality of a glass.

"Who the devil are you?" he demanded without ceremony.

"I am looking for the pit," I began, suppressing my relief at finding a living soul at last.

"The pit, is it?" He laughed unpleasantly. "Keep going in this direction and you'll find the pit, all right."

"I meant the orch—"

"I know what you meant, imbecile. Follow me." He brushed roughly past me on the narrow platform and signed for me to follow him with a gesture of the bottle. He walked with a rapidity which proclaimed his utter familiarity with his surroundings, and after what seemed like five minutes, we regained the original spiral staircase.

"Up three flights and to your left."

"Thank you. I had assumed the—"

"Don't assume anything around here or you'll never be heard from again," he advised, taking a pull on the bottle. "You're new here?"

"Today is my first rehearsal."

He grunted at this.

"Don't assume," he repeated. "Do you know how many cellars this place has?" Before I could answer, he went on. *"Five."*

"Five?" I could not keep the astonishment from my voice.

"That's right, five. This place is as deep as it is high. There's even a lake down there," he added with a hiccough.

I dismissed this intelligence as having been informed by alcohol and thanked the man again, eager not to be late. It occurred to me, as I hurried along, that morale in this place, if it was to be judged by the terrified violinist, Jérôme the doorkeeper, or the sot who had just directed my steps, was not particularly high.

I later discovered that my aged rescuer was a "door shutter," of which the Opéra boasted ten. These pensioners were retained by a charitable management at a less than modest rate, for the sole purpose of going about the house and closing every open door they chanced upon, of which, I need hardly state, there were hundreds.

This time I found the orchestra and contrived to be sitting amongst the first violins before Leroux made his appearance. I had just time to introduce myself to my neighbors on either side, a young man in his early thirties on my right with pale blue eyes, who called himself Ponelle and who welcomed me with a warm smile, and a bald individual of sixty on my left with a fierce moustache, who frowned briefly in my direction before returning to his violin, whose D-string appeared to be causing him considerable difficulty. His name, I gathered, was Bela. As his name indicated, he was of Hungarian extraction, and he seemed less than pleased to see me.

Leroux rapidly ascended the podium and bade us a gruff good morning.

"First violins have been joined by Monsieur Henrik Sigerson," he announced, gesturing in my direction with a sweep of his broad arm. I nodded. Leroux attached a gold pince-nez to the bridge of his nose (it depended from his neck on a frayed silken ribbon which had lost its color) and began flipping the pages of the score before him. I seized the opportunity to unpack my instrument and give it hasty tuning. The music was the ballet from Act III of *Le Prophète*—the ice-skating music.

"What did you think of Daaé last evening?" Leroux seemed to address his question to the brass, continuing to thumb his score.

"Astonishing," said a voice from the trombones. There was some laughter at this, the implication being that such a performance had not been anticipated from the young soprano.

"I cannot make heads or tails of it," Leroux confessed in agreement. "The most uneven temperament. Sometimes she simply goes through the motions; at others . . ." He let the sentence trail off into an eloquent shrug.

"La Sorelli must look to her laurels," suggested the percussion.

"Who asked you?" The conductor rounded on the voice with vehemence. Before the man could answer, he rapped insistently on the rostrum with his baton. "*Entr'acte!* One, two . . ."

And we were off. It had been years since I had done extensive sight-reading and I was now hard pressed to follow along and make my presence worthwhile, but my fingers were nimble from constant practice, and, as it has been observed, the whole thing is not so different from riding a bicycle—once you have learned you do not forget.

Leroux was a painstaking taskmaster with ears in the back of his head. I cannot pretend the music of Meyerbeer was especially profound, but it was well written and the conductor was determined to wring every detail from it. I found the rehearsal exhilarating and was amazed at how the time flew. We worked the passage for the better part of an hour. There was then a ten-minute interval during which time we were permitted to stretch our legs before we were joined by the *corps de ballet* onstage above us. From my chair I could see little of their antics, but these were evidently high-spirited girls, for I heard their giggles and the exuberant slicing sounds made by their skates as they whirled about on the ice above us.

"Jammes, get back where you belong!" Leroux shouted at one of them, leading us the while with an insistent hand.

"Sorry! I don't know what came over me," cried a childish voice. Jammes, I later learned, was but fifteen.

"Must have been the Ghost," muttered Ponelle to my right, his articulation somewhat strangled by the violin tucked beneath his chin. Bela frowned at this. It was evident that Bela regarded the Ghost as no laughing matter. As for myself, Ponelle's pleasantry and Bela's reaction to it I put down as yet one more of the Opéra's quaint details, which no doubt would be made clear to me in due course, as I became intimate with the place and learned its little ways.

By and by we were joined by another personage. A man of about fifty with a sort of patch over one eye and a sketch pad in his lap sat not far from us in the empty auditorium and busied himself, entirely ignoring, as near as I could judge, everything around him. His patch was not simply a cover for his eye, for it contained a narrow slit, allowing some light to penetrate.

"Degas," Ponelle informed me in a whisper, but the name meant nothing at the time. "Almost blind in one eye, but he still loves to paint their plump fleshy legs."

"He draws nothing but horses and whores," Bela complained, leaving me confused as to which category he felt the ballet belonged.

That night we performed *Otello* with the extraordinary de Reszke in the title role, and this was intensely satisfying, as I found Verdi's music infinitely superior to that of Meyerbeer. It was a unique perspective to watch the audience from the vantage point of the pit, and La Sorelli was a sensation as Desdemona.

Out of curiosity, I glanced at the Grand Tier and was mildly provoked to perceive that once again the same box remained empty.

And so began a most agreeable routine. Rehearsals in the mornings, performances at night, usually, but not always, led by Leroux. In the days that followed I became accustomed to the sight of the one-eyed artist sitting alone in the empty stalls or sometimes perched upon the edge of the apron itself as, with single-minded concentration, he pursued his work. He appeared to know all the girls by name, and they teased and talked to him when they thought Leroux was out of earshot.

As time passed I became more familiar with other intricacies of the Opéra, both social and physical. I learned, for example, that the Calliope, to which I heard frequent reference, was not in this case a musical instrument, but rather the nickname for the complicated gasworks that controlled the lighting of the theatre. Though theatres in England had begun to be illumined exclusively by electricity,* the Palais Garnier boasted an intricate gas-driven system which took four men to operate and existed on sublevel three below the central stage trapdoors.

I also learned that the horses I had admired during the performance of *Le Prophète* lived on sublevel four, which included a complete stable for no fewer than forty such animals and four coaches, all used exclusively to enhance productions. They gained access to the stage on a hard dirt circular ramp that ascended five flights. I am not certain they ever saw the light of day, save for excursions from the city when they were put to pasture for three weeks at a time. Fresh air reached them from vents placed for that purpose on the roof of the opera house.

During a performance of *Mondego,* a beautiful white gelding named César galloped with the eponymous hero on his back atop a stage treadmill to wild applause at the conclusion of Act I. I met Jacques, his handler, and remarked on the beast's performance, wondering that all the commotion did not cause him to shy. He laughed.

"Theatre's in his blood. He knows the opera by heart, hears the music, knows it's time for the treadmill."

Young Ponelle, the violinist to my right, proved to be my almanac in many of the matters regarding the place and its history. Once, when he pointed out to me that the chandelier hanging above the auditorium weighed almost six tons, I asked him how he chanced upon all this miscellaneous data.

"I grew up across the way as they were building," he explained, happy at the recollection. "Well, down the road, at any

*In 1887, the Savoy, built by Richard D'Oyly Carte for the operas of Gilbert and Sullivan, became the first theatre to be totally lit by electricity.

rate—in the house where Alphonsine Plessis died,'' he added with a touch of pride. ''You know, the one on which Verdi based his opera.* They started work in 1860 or thereabouts after young Garnier won the design competition. We urchins did some labor on the thing ourselves,'' he recalled fondly. ''Carrying buckets and bringing the men their lunch pails and so forth. Construction took fifteen years.''

''Fifteen!''

''Well, you mustn't count the entire time, because we were at war and then the Germans came. To this day, you know, they are very cautious here about staging Wagner.''

Imagine my disappointment, Watson. You know I dote on Wagner. He helps me introspect.

''What is the digging presently taking place outside along the Rue Scribe for?'' I demanded of him. ''More opera facilities?''

He shook his head.

''They are building an underground rail transit system—like the English.''

As a musician in the pit, my comings and goings did not, as a rule, bring me into much contact with other departments of the Opéra. I went to my station and shared the orchestra's dressing facilities; they were not situated near those of the soloists or chorus, and as I had but a restricted view of the stage itself from my chair, I saw little of the performers, still less of the performances.

---

*Alphonsine Plessis, a peasant from Normandy, called herself Marie Du Plessis when she was the mistress of Alexandre Dumas Fils. After her death of tuberculosis at the age of twenty-three (by which time she was a notorious courtesan), Dumas whipped out his novel *La Dame Aux Camélias,* in which he changed her name again to Marguerite Gauthier, in 1849. The play was a hit and in America was known for some reason as *Camille.* In 1853, Verdi changed the selfless heroine's name again, this time to Violetta Valery in his opera *La Traviata.*

I was, however, privy to the rumor mill, and from it I gleaned tidbits large and small. Jammes's mother was an interfering harridan, but Meg Giry's was "a character" and tended the boxes on the Grand Tier. Monsieur Mercier, the stage manager, had a mistress whose blond tresses were suspect, Messieurs Debienne and Poligny, the general managers (whom I had unknowingly encountered behind the deal table at my audition), were shortly to retire. Daaé had an admirer, rumored to be the Vicomte de Chagny. The Ghost had spoken again last night to Joseph Buquet, the head scene-shifter (also said to be in love with La Daaé.)

The Ghost. Of all the queer stories and chatter that came my way during those first two weeks, nothing I heard was so curious as those occasional references to the Ghost.

"He's practically an institution," Ponelle explained. "Nobody seems to know just where it started. I suppose the place is so huge and spooky down below that people naturally assume it's haunted. They say there are bodies down there," he added, in a respectful undertone, "from the days of the Commune, when this place was used as a prison."*

"They used this building as a prison?"

He nodded somberly. "And they threw the bodies in the lake."

"Then there *is* a lake?" I was surprised.

"Not that I've ever seen it, but when they were digging out the foundations, they came upon all this water—Paris is built on a bog,

---

*At the conclusion of the Franco-Prussian War in 1871, a group of radical Parisians, believing themselves betrayed by the French government responsible for the humiliating terms of the peace, retained the weapons they had used to fight Germans and occupied part of Paris in a revolutionary "Commune" in what amounted to a second siege of the city. They held out for two bloody months but eventually were annihilated.

you understand—which brought the whole undertaking to a halt. Then they hit upon the happy expedient of pumping out all the water temporarily while they paved the whole floor of the marsh-bed with concrete and bitumen and drove in the pilings for the building. Then they let the water return permanently, forming an underground lake. It took over eight months to create," he informed me with pride. "Though it doesn't follow that there's a ghost," he concluded with the ghost of a smile.

"It's not so simple," Bela countered, forever struggling with his D-string. "People have seen him. People have heard him."

"Bah. Superstition. What people? Where?"

"At the ends of passages; through the walls of dressing rooms. They say Madame Giry is intimate with him."

"You are absurd. How can one be intimate with a ghost?" demanded Ponelle impatiently.

"The whole *corps de ballet* is in love with him," Bela insisted. "Some see a shadow, some have met him in evening dress, others encounter him without a head—all adore him."

"But they all swear he is hideous."

"Of course they do. And they are in love with his hideousness. You know the story of *la belle et la bête*. The beast's ugliness exerts an irresistible fascination. Show me a woman who isn't disappointed when he becomes the handsome prince."

"It was no magic prince that drove Monsieur Frédéric from the theatre," Ponelle maintained with emphasis.

"What happened to Monsieur Frederick?" I interjected, suddenly interested.

"Well, what do you think caused him to run screaming into the street, swearing he'd never play here again?" demanded Bela. He turned to me. "How do you think you obtained your situation?"

"My playing?" I hazarded, somewhat nettled by the question.

"His *leaving*," he reminded me with a scowl. "And anyway," he went on, addressing Ponelle over my shoulder, "the management believes in the Ghost."

"The management is a pair of idiots," Ponelle snorted in return, "destined to be replaced by a new pair of idiots. That is the nature of management."

I was about to respond to this observation when our discussion was interrupted by a familiar peremptory rapping. "*Gentlemen.* Four bars from letter G, if you please."

And so the days passed. I found that in the evenings I automatically looked up at the Grand Tier. The box was invariably empty.

"Number five," Bela explained, following my gaze. "they say it is reserved for the Ghost." Overhearing this remark, Ponelle rolled his blue eyes.

All this conversation about a ghost meant little to me, as you can imagine, Watson. I have always been skeptical, to say the least, about supernatural manifestations. I suppose I was amused by the talk, but I cannot say that in my present frame of mind I gave the matter any serious thought. If the Ghost's effect on Monsieur Frédéric had been the happy agency of my present employment, I could only be grateful. I had utterly forgot the echoing, disembodied laughter I had imagined hearing when I had become lost that first day.

In any event, such contemplation as I might have devoted to the topic of the Ghost was shortly to be exploded by a thunderbolt which drove all other considerations from my brain.

At rehearsals one morning, Leroux made an announcement:

"Gentlemen, as you know, we begin work today on a new production of *Carmen*. Owing to the sudden indisposition of Mademoiselle Emma Calvé, the title role has been assumed at the last minute with gracious condescension by the American diva Mademoiselle Irene Adler."

3

A GHOST OF MY OWN

Had Leroux plunged his baton into my breast, he could hardly have produced a greater effect. Even as I felt myself swaying in my chair, the orchestra about me rose to applaud in welcome the last-minute substitute. I had the presence of mind to follow suit, whilst turning my head downwards, as if in an attitude of reverence, praying the while that I should not be noticed.*

I needn't have worried. Miss Adler took her bows from upstage, whence I was invisible, and shortly the rehearsal commenced in earnest.

Carmen had been written by Georges Bizet for the Opéra Comique in 1875, where its premier had been a *succès de scandale,* its

---

*To Holmes, Irene Adler was always *the* woman. For full details of their encounter, the reader is advised to consult Watson's history of the affair, labeled "A Scandal in Bohemia."

unfortunate author dying three months later at the age of thirty-five. Three months after that, his masterpiece had triumphed in Vienna and thence around the world. Paris had turned its back on *Carmen* for ten years, as if by ignoring it the sensational piece might somehow disappear. There was, however, scant likelihood of that, when such disparate personalities as Brahms, Tchaikovsky, Nietzsche, and Wagner—men who couldn't abide one another—staunchly championed as one the genius of Georges Bizet. All agreed that it was Bizet's music that elevated and indeed redeemed the lurid tale of a thieving gypsy sordidly stabbed by her jealous lover. When the French finally deigned to pay attention to what had become the most popular opera ever written, they insisted on eliminating the spoken dialogue, and one Ernest Guiraud, a "friend" of the late composer, was commissioned to replace these "offensive" passages with recitative. This treacly substitution now qualified Bizet's creation as "grand opera," hence its belated inclusion in the repertoire of the Palais Garnier.

I reminded myself of these facts while sight-reading the prelude, hoping thereby to reduce the palpitations racking my breast. Irene Adler! Can you imagine, Watson? This creature, whose back I believed I had beheld for good years ago, now returned like Lazarus. What the deuce was she doing here? Was she not married and living in retirement? Evidently not. It would have been bad enough to encounter the woman in normal circumstances, but to find her in this setting compounded my confusion and my difficulties. I had managed—for the time, at any rate—to carve out a different life for myself, and now that life was threatened by the reappearance of my old and successful adversary.

How could I hope to avoid her? Take sick leave? This seemed poorly advised; I had, after all, only recently assumed my duties, and Maître Leroux would hardly countenance an absence that lasted the length of the run.

As I played, I grew calmer. I reflected that since Miss Adler could not see into the pit from the stage and since the artistes' dressing rooms—eighty in number!—were separate from those of the orchestra, I might successfully manage to avoid her altogether.

Soon, however, we were launched into the "Habañera" and I was subject to a new torment. I had, of course, heard reports of Miss Adler's voice—she was celebrated at La Scala as well as at the Warsaw Imperial Opera—but until now her singing had only reached my ears by repute. Now, exposed to the real thing, I could but own that the critics had underrated her gifts. Concentrating on her great beauty, the press had neglected or been unable to describe the richness of her tone. She has been called a contralto, but in truth, she was a mezzo, the range for which *Carmen* was originally written (though sopranos insisted on essaying the role with transpositions upwards).

It was a species of torture that a Torquemada might have devised. Invisible beneath her, I was compelled to listen to that siren voice as she played the part of a siren and seduced Don José, day after day in rehearsal, and left to anticipate the prospect of her being murdered by him, night after night when we opened.

The premiere was everything the Paris Opéra stood for and could have wished. The encores were endless, and the same Parisians who had scorned Bizet's earthy adaptation of the novella by Prosper Merimée sixteen years before now cheered Miss Adler's interpretation of Merimée's quintessential Gypsy to the rafters. I could swear the chandelier itself shook with their bravos. And although I could not see her, hearing her seductive voice in the role reminded me that she was an actress *sans pareille.**

---

*Irene Adler was not the only American to triumph in Europe in the role. Parisians were also mad for Minnie Hauk as Carmen.

Audiences are mercifully ignorant of the chaos that proceeds backstage during a theatrical production. They remain blissfully unaware of missed cues, broken props, confusion between the singers and the conductor, and the whole host of minor calamities which invariably distinguish every performance. There are simply too many possibilities for things to go wrong, but the frantic shouts and furious whispers behind the scenes rarely reach the ears of those who come for the music.

Not so for those of us in the pit. During our first *Carmen,* something did occur backstage during Act II, for I heard screams and cries during the second interval, but separated from the source of the confusion in the orchestra's dressing rooms on the opposite side of the theatre, we were unable to learn what had happened. From a distance and lost in a welter of competing sound, it was impossible to make out the import of the noise. Before rumors had time to reach us, the opera resumed and the matter was forced from my consciousness by my musical responsibilities and by other more pressing considerations.

There was to be a reception following the performance, which we were all expected to attend. This function I was most desirous to avoid, since I knew our Carmen would be there. So far I had contrived to elude her notice, and nothing had occurred to warrant my altering this arrangement. Almost before the final curtain, therefore, I fairly leapt from my chair and made my escape. Normally, after changing into my street clothing, I retired to a nearby bar on the Rue Madeleine with Ponelle and sometimes Bela for a sandwich and a glass of cognac before heading home; tonight such camaraderie was eschewed. Still in evening dress, I hastened to the Marais, drank off my cognac at a corner bistro, and then headed for my lodgings, where I planned to stare at the ceiling.

Outside my apartments as I approached them, a tall, slender youth lounged against the building, a wide, soft-brimmed hat pulled down rakishly over one eye.

"Good evening, Monsieur Sigerson."

I was on the point of brushing past with a muttered response when I heard a snatch of the "Sequidilla" in a throaty mezzo which caused me to whirl about. The youth laughed, displaying a set of perfect teeth and flashing dark eyes. It was Carmen herself.

"Miss Adler!"

"I see you have grown more acute since our last encounter."*

I glanced hastily about me at the shadowy street.

"How did you learn I was here?"

"I will answer that question and others if you will have the goodness to show me your rooms," she replied, thrusting herself off the wall. "Come," she went on, seeing me hesitate, "you have nothing to fear from me. I am and always was quite harmless."

Rather than dispute this statement where others might overhear our altercation, I drew forth my latchkey and led her upstairs.

Inside my spare digs (which abruptly struck me as being almost squalid), Irene Adler tossed aside her hat, drew off her gloves, circled the place like a cat, and finally settled herself in a chair—the sole one, opposite my sofa—and crossed her trousered legs. Time, it seemed, was hers to command. She was as beautiful as the photograph I had treasured for years, and which now reposed in solitary splendor on the mantel. Her skin remained flawless as cream with a rosy tint, her lustrous eyes were wonderfully alert above humorous, pouting lips, and her shining hair still gleamed like burnished ebony. Her beauty indeed was almost painful to behold, for I was

---

*At which time, again in man's dress, she bade Holmes good night and he failed to detect her beneath the disguise.

aware as I studied her of a faint throbbing at my temples. You know how unaccustomed I am to headaches, Watson.

"Have you nothing to drink?"

"I'm afraid not." I stared at her inhospitably, but she returned my gaze with an even regard.

"Please sit, Monsieur Sigerson. We have much to discuss."

I sank into my sofa, irritated by the fashion in which she appeared to be controlling this interview.

"You may imagine my surprise," I began, hoping to retrieve the initiative. "I was under the impression you were married and retired."

"Mr. Norton died of influenza within a year of our marriage,"* she responded in a low tone, averting her gaze momentarily, "and I was obliged to resume my career for financial reasons."

"I am sorry to learn of your loss," I said, and meant it. I noticed she still wore her wedding ring. "And sorry, as well, to learn of your financial difficulties."

She shrugged philosophically at this, as one who has seen and is unfazed by adversity.

"My head is still above water, as we say in my country.† And I expect I have a few good years left," she added with a pause that invited me to comment.

"Based on what I have been hearing day after day," I responded sincerely, "I see no end for your triumphs."

"You are too kind."

"But you have not told me how you knew I was here."

She smiled, and her gaze flickered briefly in the direction of her photograph.

---

*Miss Adler married a London lawyer of the Inner Temple, Godfrey Norton, in 1887. Holmes (in disguise) was a witness at the ceremony.

†Miss Adler's country was New Jersey. She was born in Hoboken, the birthplace of at least one other major singer.

"Do you know what divas do to occupy their time between performances?"

"Are you certain you are quite prepared to tell me?"

She ignored the gibe, staring at the toe of her boot as she swung it negligently to and fro. My headache was worsening.

"We two are men of the world, are we not?" she laughed. "I think I dare take you into my confidence. Divas tour the strange cities in which they find themselves. They visit monuments and museums; they go to art galleries."

"I am afraid I do not follow."

"I was at the Galerie du Monde some days ago," she explained, "looking at a series of pastels and watercolors by Monsieur Degas."

"Oh?"

"Imagine my surprise when staring at a series of ballerinas sketched at the Opéra, I saw your face in the pit beneath them, playing the violin!"*

I could only gape at her. Seeing this, she laughed again.

"You may imagine that I found it hard to believe. Degas is, after all, what they call an Impressionist.† Yet the impression was a distinct one. Who could mistake that aquiline profile, the hawklike nose, the hooded eyes and intellectual brow? And who, from reading Dr. Watson's accounts, could fail to remember your proficiency on a Stradivarius? When I recalled that you had been declared officially dead, my mind was set to working overtime as I stared at the picture. There could be no doubt. I did not trouble myself as to why you were in Monsieur Degas's drawing, nor did I consider exposing

---

*Holmes by Degas! This priceless pastel formed until recently part of the collection of the late Baron Von Thurm und Taxis Von Thyssen. It was auctioned to an anonymous bidder by Von Thyssen's widow in Geneva in 1992, as part of an effort to pay the late Baron's death duties.

†"Impressionist" was still a term of disparagement in 1891.

you, for very shortly I felt I should have need of your services. I merely made a few discreet inquiries at the Opéra and discovered your alias.''

''My reasons for remaining incognito are my own,'' I responded carefully. ''But it would not do for the criminal element to learn I am alive until it suits me.''

''You may depend on me to respect your wishes.'' She sat there in friendly silence, waiting, as I realized, for me to rejoin her. It seemed that in my dealings with this person, I was forever destined to lag behind. My temples throbbing painfully, I now recalled the rest of her previous sentence.

''What services?''

''Were you aware of a commotion backstage this evening?''

''I heard something.''

''There was a suicide.''

''A suicide?''

''I will give you the details as they are known to me. Have you a cigarette? Playing this role, I fear, has given me a taste for tobacco.''

I produced my case and offered her one, suppressing any expression of disapproval. I had the feeling that if I remonstrated she would only laugh at me and claim some sort of ''bohemian'' privilege, relishing the *double entendre*.

''Whose suicide?''

She accepted a light and located an ashtray before answering.

''The chief scene-shifter, Joseph Buquet. He was found hanging from a rope during Act II, in the third cellar beneath the stage.''

''Ah.''

''No doubt you were aware that something occurred during tonight's performance?''

''We heard a disturbance, yes.''

I found that I had settled into my accustomed position when

listening to a client who was providing me with the background of a case, my fingers pressed together, my eyes closed, the better to avoid distractions.

"Well, now you know the cause of that disturbance."

"It is unfortunate," I heard myself say, "but seems hardly to warrant my attention."

"Are you familiar with Christine Daaé?" she asked, instead of responding directly.

"I am familiar with her voice. We have never had occasion to meet."

"She is my friend." I opened my eyes at this and saw hers twinkling with amusement. "Oh, I know what the public like to think and what the papers encourage them to think—terrible rivalries between prima donnas, hair-pulling matches behind the scenes, and so forth." She shook her head. "But rarely, I think, between a mezzo and a coloratura. We are not in direct competition. No," she went on, putting out her cigarette with a reflective air, "I have no grudge with little Christine. On the contrary, I feel distinctly protective towards her. I have taken her beneath my wing."

"Indeed?"

"There are people in this world, Monsieur Sigerson, who have but one gift. Some are thinking machines . . ." She trailed off with a smile, and I inclined my head. "Others have different specialties—or should I say, limitations."

"And Mademoiselle Daaé?"

"She is quite an innocent, you will be interested to learn. Beautiful and simple—one might almost be tempted to say simpleminded. She is an orphan from Scandinavia, taught her music by a widowed father, now himself deceased. She knows little of life, only her music. And she cannot conceive of the machinations of a sophisticated world in which she finds herself at present the center."

"You refer to the Vicomte de Chagny?"

She raised her eyebrows.

"You have sharp ears."

"Come, come, madame. Backstage one hears almost everything whether one is listening or not."

"The young man is certainly in love with her, but he is not the only one."

"Who else, then?"

"Joseph Buquet."

For the second time my eyes opened. This time I did not find hers smiling at me.

"The scene-shifter? Yes, I did hear something of the sort, now you mention it. He was aiming rather high if he thought to set his cap for Mademoiselle Daaé."

"That was the view taken by the young Vicomte, who discovered him in her dressing room, on his knees protesting his devotion."

"I take it there was a scene?"

She gave an imperceptible shrug of her elegant shoulders.

"I could hear it quite plainly from my own dressing room, which lies next to hers. The Vicomte threw Buquet out of Christine's room and quitted the Opéra himself directly afterwards in the company of his elder brother, the Comte, leaving my poor friend in hysterics. I heard such details as I have shared with you when I went to comfort her."

"And subsequently Buquet did away with himself?"

"Apparently."

"What do you mean?"

"After the body was discovered—"

"Who discovered it? Pray be precise as to particulars where you can."

"It was found by two other members of the scene-shifting crew. I do not know their names. They raised a great cry—I could hear it quite clearly during the 'Flower Song'—and others, including Debienne and Poligny, the managers"—I nodded, familiar with these men—"rushed to help cut the wretched man down. But when they had returned to the sight of the tragedy, what do you imagine they found?"

"Imagination is not my strong suit. I prefer to deal in facts."

She nodded, conceding the point.

"They found the poor man's body already on the floor—and the rope from which he had been hanging had vanished."

"Vanished?"

"That is to say, he had already been cut down. Half the rope was still attached to the beam beneath which his body had been discovered. It had been slashed. Buquet was on the floor, but the rest of the rope, the part that had been around his neck, had disappeared."

"Perhaps it had been removed by one of the other scene-shifters."

"They thought at first that might be the case. But as the area had been sealed following the discovery and a guard stationed at the only door leading to the third cellar, it would have been impossible for it to have been taken. In the event, all denied having touched the body."

"And yet . . ."

"Just so. Where is the rope?" She rose with an apprehensive air and took a turn about the small room as I watched. "They have summoned the police, of course, but I have some experience of officialdom and I do not hold out much hope. More to the point, I am, as I say, worried for my friend. She seems somehow to be at the center of an intrigue which swirls about her but of which she is ignorant, no more responsible for what happens than a candle is for the moths which hover and dive about it until they are fatally singed.''

"Are there other moths?"

She hesitated, a petite frown joining her delicate eyebrows above the ridge of her nose.

"There is a man. . . ." She paused.

"Go on." She looked at me quizzically, then threw herself back into the chair with a sigh.

"But I have never seen him."

"Oh?"

"Her dressing room is next to mine, as I have said. I can hear them—not specific words, you understand, merely the drone of their conversation. Her voice, then his, then hers." She trailed off with a vague wafture of her fingers. "Sometimes I fancy he is her singing master, for I hear them singing."

"Really."

She nodded.

"That is curious."

"So I thought."

"But hardly exceptional in an opera house. Perhaps he is her coach."

"She has none that I know of. I expect she would have mentioned him to me if there were one, for that is the sort of thing we discuss."

"You say you hear them singing. Do you mean duets?"

"Sometimes. On other occasions she sings and then I hear him speak in low tones, as if he were commenting on her performance. Of course, that may be merely my impression."

I nodded.

"Have you ever had occasion to refer to this gentleman when you speak with Mademoiselle Daaé?"

"That would hardly be discreet," she replied reasonably. "Tell me," she added, sitting up and smiling, "have you heard about the phantom of the Opéra?"

"He is on everyone's lips. Every practical joke, every missed cue, is ascribed to his agency."

"Some people believe he exists."

"Mademoiselle Daaé, for example?"

"She will not own to it, but she does. In addition, Madame Giry, mother of little Meg, who tends the boxes on the Grand Tier left, is also convinced."

"Has she ever seen him?"

"No, but she has heard his voice."

"Voices again. I think perhaps we are wandering rather far afield," I suggested. "I am not an exorcist."

"I wish you to protect Christine," Irene Adler said bluntly. "When La Calvé recovers, which will not be long, she will resume my role and I will be on my way to fulfill other engagements. As it happens, I am due in Amsterdam in four days' time. I wish you to protect Christine," she repeated with finality, as if assuring herself on this point. "The Vicomte may love her, but he is a mere puppy himself, another novice of the world's devices, like his mistress."

"And if I refuse?"

She stopped pacing and regarded her photograph on the mantel with an inscrutable expression, her head cocked to one side.

"Should you refuse . . ." She hesitated, speaking again as if to herself. ". . . I suppose I should be forced to reconsider the matter of my silence regarding your incognito."

"I forget that blackmail was your specialty."*

---

*In "A Scandal in Bohemia," Holmes believed Irene Adler to be black-mailing the king of Bohemia, an accusation which proved only half true.

"Always in a worthy cause," she amended, not at all put out. "Your fee shall be my silence."

I sat and tried to think through the numbness of my headache, while she affected to examine her finger ends.

"How am I to insinuate myself into a portion of the backstage community with which I normally have no contact?" I demanded. "I can hardly go about in disguise and still maintain my place in the orchestra."

"I have given the matter some thought. There is a farewell party backstage this evening in honor of Messieurs Poligny and Debienne, who, as I take it you are aware, are retiring as managing directors of the Opéra. I am certain it has only just got underway. You are still in evening dress and will escort me. I shall introduce you as a friend from my days at the Oslo Royal Opera. In this way you can become acquainted with Christine and many of the principals in this affair."

"Will this reception not be cancelled in view of what has occurred?"

"Surely, Monsieur Sigerson, you are aware of the maxim which assures us that the show must go on?"

"I am in evening dress, but you are not," I pointed out, rising reluctantly and retrieving my cloak.

"I am, as always, an exception." She smiled, fetching her own outer garments. "In the land of George Sand and Sarah Bernhardt, my mode of sartorial expression will be tolerated, if not understood, the more especially in an artist. Shall we go?"

I had no choice.

4

FIRST BLOOD

*T*he reception, when we reached it in another of those enormous greenrooms, was rather a subdued affair. It was nevertheless one of those situations which, for the moment, enforces a false *bonhomie,* a specious democracy, cutting across the class divisions and distinctions backstage, in which the managers pretend to mingle on terms of perfect equality with the ladies who show folk to their seats, wardrobe mistresses rub shoulders with musicians, and tenors get to flirt with the *corps de ballet,* who are only interested in gorging themselves at the buffet.

La Sorelli was in a corner, rehearsing her farewell speech to the retiring managers and assisting her memory with a tapered glass of champagne and a bottle next to it.

Leroux held court in another portion of the room, attended by members of the ensemble, who hung on his every word. He

looked like a man who, given the choice between boring himself or boring others, had unhesitatingly adopted the latter course.

Christine Daaé was not present. The death of Buquet and the terrible scene in her dressing room which had preceded it had so unnerved the young soprano that a doctor had placed her under sedation and seen to it that she was taken home.

My entrance with Irene Adler on my arm—in male attire, no less—caused something of a sensation, and I could see my stock rising amongst the company by virtue of our association. Those who had dismissed me as simply another cog in the great machinery of the Opéra were now busy reevaluating my status. Mercifully, now that I had work to distract me, my headache was on the wane.

"Sigerson, you're a sly bit of business," Ponelle exclaimed, taking me to one side. "You let none of us know you were acquainted with Mademoiselle Adler."

"I am a professional," I temporized and, in response to an impatient gesture from my hostess, left him to his conjectures.

She presented me to Debienne and Poligny, with whom I had not spoken since my first interview. These gentlemen did not trouble to question my bona fides as an old friend of Irene Adler's from the Oslo Opera, for they were engaged in a heated discussion with little Jammes, Meg Giry, and her mother, all of whom had earlier been interviewed by Monsieur Mifroid of the Paris prefecture. An excited chorus of exclamation and horror accompanied their conversation, with little Jammes insisting that only the Ghost could be held responsible for Buquet's death and Meg Giry enthusiastically endorsing this view.

"I have seen himself myself," she preened, happy to be the center of the attention which followed this statement.

"What? When?"

"I was the last one down the ladder during the final perform-

ance of *Le Prophète,* and he was standing at the end of the corridor, lit by the sole lamp next to the cellar door. He was in evening dress.''

''He is always in evening dress,'' another voice contributed.

''What did he do?'' demanded another.

''He bowed low in my direction and disappeared into the wall! I was never so frightened in my life.''

''And his face?'' demanded a third.

''Horrible! A death's head!'' This intelligence was greeted by a collective gasp. ''Yes, a death's head,'' Meg reiterated, clearly satisfied by the response she had elicited.

''Joseph claimed to have seen him,'' interrupted Jammes, eager to compete for center stage and retrieve the spotlight for herself. Instantly the crowd reconfigured itself about Meg's rival.

''Buquet? Are you certain?''

''He told me so himself,'' the imp insisted. ''He said the face had no face—there was no nose or mouth, only dark flashing eyes.''

''Well, that settles it,'' another concluded. ''It must have been the Ghost that killed him.''

This statement, which rather brought the discussion to a halt, was not disputed by the management.

''Where exactly was the unfortunate man's body found?'' I asked, attempting to present a casual demeanor. They might not have troubled to answer my question but for my newfound significance as an intimate of Mademoiselle Adler.

''Between a set piece and a statue from *Le Roi de Lahore,*'' said Poligny, shaking his head at the memory of it.

''Was this Buquet the sort of fellow likely to do away with himself?''

Someone sniggered.

''He'd much sooner do away with *you.*''

The management agreed.

"Buquet was not a man to take things lying down." The silence that followed implied one explanation only.

"And do I take it you gentlemen believe in the Ghost?"

"We know he exists."

"May one inquire how you know?"

They looked at each other briefly, uncertain whether to pursue the topic in this public arena. Madame Giry spoke up instead.

"I tend his box, monsieur," she announced with lofty condescension in a voice designed to include the group. I could see where the daughter came by her egocentricity.

"Box five?"

"Why yes, how did you—?"

I brushed aside her question with a little laugh.

"And how do you know he occupies the box if you have never seen him?"

"Oh, but he always leaves me three francs tip."

"A considerate ghost," I was forced to admit.

"And he has given strict orders the box is to be reserved for him at all times."

"You have heard him?"

"Through the walls, monsieur. He has the sweetest voice in all the world."

I looked at Poligny and Debienne, but they affected not to have listened to this interchange and busied themselves at the buffet.

The soirée went on and speculations about the death of the unfortunate scene-shifter resumed. The grisly affair exerted a fascination which was too recent for the company to resist. I took Irene Adler by the elbow and led her gently away from the center of the conversation.

"I should like to examine the site of Buquet's alleged suicide,"

I explained in an undertone. "If my absence is noticed, would you make my excuses?"

She nodded, and when La Sorelli began her speech extolling Debienne and Poligny, celebrating and bidding farewell to their administration, I quietly slipped from the room.

Before making my descent, I made it my business to locate and examine the empty dressing room of Christine Daaé. It was an unexceptional if spacious accommodation, walled with looking glass and boasting a folding screen akin to the one that had shielded me from Leroux at my audition. A sink, a wardrobe containing several costumes, a bureau, a revolving stool, and a divan completed the spare appointments. A delicate fragrance pervaded the chamber, doubtless the scent of Mademoiselle Daaé's eau de toilette.

I was not certain what I hoped to learn by this examination, but the room suggested nothing to me. I was rusty, Watson. In addition, I was deprived of the resources normally available to me. In London, I should have been able to question the men who found Buquet, to have examined the body; in a word, to have amassed such trifles as I needed to construct my chain of evidence. Here was no such luxury. In effect, one hand had been tied behind my back. However, there was nothing for it but to work with such means as were left at my disposal.

Quitting the dressing room, I climbed back to the entry hall and thence made my way to the spiral staircase at the end of it, where I hesitated, feeling rather like Alice about to pop down the rabbit hole.

Mindful of the fact that I had been lost before in the subterranean expanse, I paid strict attention to my route as I commenced my descent.

Very quickly I left behind the sounds of the reception. Cheers

and toasts following La Sorelli's valedictory faded into stillness as I made my way below.

At what I took to be the third landing, I seized a large bull's-eye lantern from the sconce by the stair and stepped towards the set piece, where I at once recognized the statue from *Le Roi de Lahore*. Above me in the darkness was the beam from which poor Buquet had swung. Shrouded in shadow I could yet make out a length of beige hemp and a neat angular slice at the lower end. The police examination was evidently incomplete, for they had not yet removed the rope fragment.

I had but faint illumination and no magnifying glass, Watson; nevertheless, you know my methods. I fell to the ground and proceeded to attempt an examination of the site. As I feared, the place yielded little. Too many feet had pattered about the area recently, scuffing the dust and shredding the cobwebs, which had the effect of obscuring what I might have learned.

As it was, the site and circumstances were susceptible of more than one interpretation. While no one at the upstairs reception seemed to think Joseph Buquet capable of suicide, there was nevertheless no direct evidence to rule out the possibility. Was it not even conceivable that the "Ghost" (for want of another title, that one must serve), far from being Buquet's murderer, had in fact attempted his rescue, discovering and cutting down the hapless scene-shifter while his associates were off raising the alarm and summoning help? This too might explain the body's being on the floor when they returned.

Why, then, had he removed the rope from the dead man's neck?

I was on the point of abandoning my efforts and rising to my feet when a violent blow to the back of my head knocked me almost unconscious, scattering the lamp from my grip and plunging the place into near darkness.

Before I could collect my senses, a pair of strong arms seized me from behind and pulled me to the ground again, cutting off my windpipe in the process. I rolled over in an attempt to shed my hidden assailant, but he went with me, never loosening his iron grip. His cloak enveloped us both as we twisted and careered back and forth across the concrete, and I could hear him sobbing for breath close to my right ear. My eyes rolled up in their sockets for want of air, as I began to lapse into unconsciousness.

Realizing that the situation called for desperate measures, I engaged my knowledge of baritsu* and tossed him over my shoulder, where he landed with a crunching sound and exclamation. If this was the Ghost, he had bones.

Feeling about me in the dark, I recovered the lantern and relit it before getting to my feet and stumbling over to my assailant.

"May I ask to whom I owe the honor?" I said, panting.

He uncurled himself with difficulty, groaning the while, then squinted up at me, licking a split lip.

"Are you the Ghost?" he demanded.

"Are *you?*"

"I, monsieur, am Vicomte Raoul de Chagny."

I extended a hand to the second son of one of the most ancient families in France. He grasped it reluctantly, and I pulled him to his feet. In the light from the stair above, I saw he was but a boy, not more than eighteen, his face dirty and frightened.

"What are you doing in this place?"

"I might ask you the same question," he countered, still catching his breath.

"I believe circumstances give me the right to act as interlocutor," I insisted gently. "Why did you attack me?"

*The ancient Japanese art of wrestling of which Holmes was a master (see "The Adventure of the Empty House"). The discipline is so arcane that I have been unable to locate any living practitioners.

"Are you not another of her lovers?"

"Whose?"

"Christine's! Did I not follow you to her dressing room?"

I stared at him blankly for a moment and resisted the impulse to laugh. It struck me that the young man was even more out of his depth than I. Any lingering thoughts of chastisement were driven from my mind by the sorry and disheveled figure he cut. Come to that, we had both been made ridiculous by the fell clutch of circumstance.

"Where did you go after your fight with Buquet?" I inquired.

"That rascal—" the other began.

"Vicomte," I pressed, "please answer my question. Where were you during tonight's performance?"

He sighed, and I watched him brush off his clothing with a shamefaced, rueful air.

"My brother does not approve of what he refers to as my infatuation. He collected me here after my—outburst and insisted I join him for supper at Maxim's. I have only just returned to find her gone."

"Do you know why she has gone?"

"I have no idea."

"Monsieur le Vicomte," said I at length, "I believe you could use a drink."

5

THE VICOMTE'S STORY

It has been said that if one stops long enough at that cross-roads of the world known as the Café de la Paix, it is only a matter of time before one encounters an acquaintance. This was just the sort of circumstance I hoped to avoid. Nevertheless, I had to yield to the little Vicomte in the matter of which bar was to dispense our libation. As in a duel, wherein the challenger surrenders the preference of weapons, the young man assumed that it was his prerogative to select the site of our drink. As he was accustomed to all the haunts of the *haut monde* and used only to the best, I should not have been astonished at his choice. It caused me some unease, however, and I kept my head lowered towards my cognac. Outside, through the corner window, I could make out six steam shovels on the Rue Scribe standing idle, like ghostly sentinels resting from their labors on the Paris Underground that was to be.

For his part, de Chagny contented himself with an absinthe, which he drank off at a gulp before commanding another.

"Dead, you say?"

In as few words as possible, I had related the events which had succeeded his exit from the theatre earlier in the evening. His only response was to order yet another round.

"Am I under suspicion?" he demanded suddenly, his latest drink halfway to his bruised lips.

"Your alibi would seem to preclude that possibility," I informed him, but he seemed far from reassured.

"I didn't kill the man, in heaven's name. Don't you know who I am?" he resumed indignantly.

I was tired. I answered before I thought.

"Beside your ancestry and the fact that you are a recent graduate of the École Naval,* now awaiting passage on the *Requin*, bound for the Arctic Circle in search of survivors from the *D'Artois* expedition, I know little. You have an elder brother with whom you are on good terms, but—"

He was staring at me, open-mouthed.

"So you *have* been following me!"

"What? No, I assure you," I began, groping for a plausible explanation. "It is part of the new science of deduction," I interposed before he could interrupt again, "of which I have made a small study."

"The science of *what*?"

"I observe you, and what do I see? I see a young man with a carriage so erect as to proclaim his military training; that you are in the navy is evident when I perceive you have somewhat impetuously had an anchor tattooed on your left hand; that you are a lieutenant is evident to me from the handkerchief you carry in your sleeve

---

*The French Naval Academy, located in Lamvic Toulmic.

instead of your breast pocket, as well as the signet ring on the fourth finger of your right hand. Though you are in mufti rather than uniform, you persist in wearing your cap indoors as is the naval custom. Clearly you are not on duty, yet neither are you ill. On extended furlough, then, but why? Why, I ask myself, does this young lieutenant have so much time on his hands? He is waiting to ship out, evidently, but his orders have not come through. What could it be that is taking so long? I read in the papers of delays surrounding the outfitting of the *Requin* for her forthcoming passage to the Arctic and make so bold as to infer that this is your duty and your destination."

He stared at me some more.

"Science of deduction." Suddenly his features brightened and he snapped his fingers. "Oh, I see, like Dupin!"

"Who?"

"You know, Auguste Dupin, the famous French detective."

I was on the point of allowing my irritation at this idiotic remark to remove what was left of my incognito but thought better of it and had a second cognac instead.*

"Who are you, then?" he pursued, ordering yet another absinthe.

"A violinist."

"Oh."

"Who may be able to help you with Mademoiselle Daaé," I found myself saying.

"She refuses to speak to me," he mumbled. I understood my time was limited if I was to extract data from him whilst he remained coherent.

"How did you come to meet the lady?"

---

*Holmes scorned Dupin as "a very inferior fellow"—see *A Study in Scarlet*.

"Well," he drawled, "as you have inferred, I am here waiting to board the *Requin*. We have had endless problems with our suppliers of arctic equipment, and, as you may imagine, my captain is not anxious to suffer the same fate as that which overtook the *D'Artois*. And so I wait." He shrugged, as one accustomed to setbacks of this sort. "My brother, Philippe, brought me to the opera a month ago, by way of distraction. I do not know anything about music to speak of, but oh, monsieur—"

"Sigerson."

"Monsieur Sigerson, how that girl captured my soul the moment I looked upon her! The moment I heard her, for truly she trills like a canary." He blushed to the roots of his hair. "These are not the proper musical terms, I know."

"Never mind the terms. Go on. You met the young woman?"

"I insisted. I sent flowers and my card. She consented to see me. I told her she had bewitched me. For her part, she led me to believe she was not insensible to my affections, but . . . ."

"But what?"

"She is so damned mysterious! So innocent on the one hand, so full of secrets on the other. She swears I have no rival, but how can I be certain? I dread to think her perfidious, yet I cannot banish the thought from my brain!" At this he made a fist of one hand and smashed it into the palm of the other.

"What reason have you to doubt her? Buquet?"

He shrugged off the notion.

"I admit I found the blackguard on his knees in her dressing room this evening," he confessed, swirling a tumbler filled with liquid before him, "but I knew the intrusion was his idea, not hers, when I threw him out. Of course, I had no idea the fellow meant to do away with himself."

In his present advancing condition he appeared to have for-

gotten what I had told him the evidence suggested as to Buquet's true fate.

"Who then?"

"I will give you the most flagrant example. I went to hear her as Marguerite in *Faust*. Great heavens, how she sang! No one had ever heard such a voice; the whole place was enraptured, mad, cheering her to the heavens, which echoed with her name. Even my brother, more familiar with the singers than I, said she had never sung so well in her life. The 'Jewel Song' was beyond perfection— what genius, and how extraordinarily packaged, if you, uh, take my meaning," he concluded, blushing again.

"Where did she study, do you know?"

"That's just it—she had never studied, except with her aged father, who is now dead. No one could account for her stupendous mastery, and by the end of the evening the woman was actually *fainting* on the stage, seemingly crushed by her reception!"

"You are certain this was not, shall we say, theatrical license?"

"Do I look like a fool, monsieur?"

It seemed prudent to shake my head. The little Vicomte interrupted his narrative to signal the waiter for a fifth absinthe.

"I made my way backstage after the performance. I was directed to her dressing room, and I watched as the wardrobe woman emerged with her costume and heard her mutter to herself, 'She is not herself tonight.' I waited until she had gone. I was on the point of knocking on the door when I heard voices!"

"Her voice?"

"Yes, but also a man's! 'Christine, you must love me,' it said. And she replied, seemingly choking on her tears: 'How can you speak this way *when I sing only for you?*' " The young Vicomte clutched his heart at the memory. "I thought I should expire on the spot, but there was more. 'Are you very tired?' the voice de-

manded. 'Oh, tonight I gave you my soul and I am dead!' she told him. 'Your soul is a beautiful thing, child,' said the voice, speaking with infinite tenderness, 'and I thank you. No Caesar received so fair a gift. The angels wept this night.' "

"Can you describe the voice you heard? The man's voice?"

"Oh, monsieur, it was the loveliest voice I had ever heard, save hers, so filled with sweetness and longing! 'The angels wept this night'!"

The Vicomte's face streamed hot tears now, as he stared at his empty glass and recollected those terrible words.

"What did you do then?" I prompted gently.

"I waited for him to come out, that's what," he said defiantly, looking me blearily in the eye and daring me to find fault with him. "I determined to confront my rival and administer a thrashing, or else challenge him to a duel," he added with a touch of uncertainty.

"But he didn't come out, that's the wonder of it, monsieur! Eventually the door opened and Christine emerged in her wrap, quite alone. I was hidden by this time, and she did not see me but hastened down the corridor. When she had gone, I raced into her dressing room. She had turned off the gas and I found myself in darkness. 'I know you are here!' I called, thrusting myself against the door and leaning my full weight against it. 'And you shall not leave this room until you reveal yourself!' But there was no sound except the beating of my own heart, the gasp of my own breath. I fumbled for the key, locked the door, and relit the gas. As I sit here before you, monsieur, *the room was entirely empty*. I went mad then, searching for him, opening the wardrobe, tearing through the clothes there, looking behind the divan—all useless. He had vanished into the air. All I could hear as I stood there, shaking, was the faint sound of music."

"Music? The performance was over, surely."

"Not from the Opéra." He made an impatient gesture with his hand.

"Where, then?"

"From . . ." He shrugged with exasperation. "Who knows where? From the air itself!"

"What kind of music? Singing?"

"Singing, yes, a man's voice, but also"—he looked at me, as if for confirmation—"an organ?"

"Close by? Distant?"

"Very distant, and very beautiful, as if it gave articulation to my inmost utterances, the very beating of my heart!"

The confession had drained him, but he had not done. He raised his eyes to mine and shook his head.

"Then came the dreadful sequel. I was quite frantic by this time, and I followed Christine home, rained blows on the door of the house where she lives with the good old woman. When she answered, I flung her treachery in her face, told her I had heard all and demanded that she tell me the name of my rival. She went dead white at my news, monsieur, almost swooned in my arms, but then became terribly angry. I did not think she could be so angry," he remembered, shaking his head. "She, so good, so pure." He paused as though gathering his resources to finish his narrative. "We had a terrible scene. She accused me of eavesdropping on a business that was no affair of mine." He cupped his hand over his mouth in an almost childlike gesture as he told me this. "When I returned home the following morning, a note awaited me—from her," he added bitterly. 'If you love me,' it ran, 'never seek to see me again.' Good Lord!"

Tears gushed from his eyes afresh and he fell sobbing on the table, his head buried in his arms, entirely oblivious to the figure he cut before the other diners. Indeed, from the look of it he would shortly be oblivious to everything. I looked around briefly and realized I must get him home somehow. I found one of his cards in the fob pocket of his waistcoat, paid the bill, and got a waiter to assist me in helping him into a cab. The man assisted me without remark, evidently familiar with and inured long since to such exhibitions amongst the café's clientele.

"Thirty-six Avenue Kléber."

I sat lost in thought on the short journey, the young man's head pressed to my shoulder as he slept stuporously. Here was a pretty kettle of fish, Watson. The canary, it seems, had a trainer, an invisible singing organist! How to proceed? Never have I been so handicapped. Again, all my instincts bade me go to the Morgue that evening and examine the corpse of Buquet, but upon what pretext could I possibly present myself? I had none of the para- phernalia of my disguises, no wigs, false noses, or spurious docu- ments with which to alter and justify my existence, indeed no case to call my own, were the truth to be told. Who was my client? A woman I had never laid eyes on? Where was my fee? Had there indeed even been a crime?

Of that, at least, I was reasonably certain. Else what had become of the rest of Buquet's rope? How I wished you were there, old friend. You are not luminous, Watson, as I have noted, but you are a conductor of light. I had no one before whom I might pro- pound my theories, and I keenly missed your reassuring presence. You have the knack, my boy, of always asking the right question, of saying the right thing and that in the right way. Now here was no one but myself to converse with my echoing thoughts.

About this missing rope one fact appeared evident: someone had cut down the miserable Buquet and absconded with it. The only question was: why? What possible difference could it make to poor Buquet whether he was left hanging by it or not?

My tired brain could think of one answer only: to inform the world that his death was no suicide. If no suicide, then murder.

And why should the chief scene-shifter be murdered? I hear you say. Elementary, my dear fellow, because he loved Christine Daaé.

The cab arrived before an imposing residence, and with some assistance from the driver, I was able to prop the little Vicomte against one of the Corinthian columns of the porte cochère whilst I drew the bell. Some moments passed before a light appeared in the foyer and the door opened to reveal a taller, stouter, older, moustachioed version of the Vicomte.

The Comte de Chagny stared at his brother and then at me with a frosty expression.

"It is late," he observed.

"Your brother has had rather too much to drink," I replied. "He has had a bad shock," I added, by way of mitigation.

The Comte hesitated a moment longer and then abruptly made up his mind.

"Henri!" he called, summoning an elderly retainer who helped the Vicomte inside, while he himself stood in the doorway, preventing my entry.

"Thank you."

"The Vicomte is in love with Mademoiselle Daaé," I ventured.

"It will pass," he assured me and shut the door in my face.

6

MY DISGUISE

Messieurs Debienne and Poligny were packing. Their offices, when I visited them the following morning, presented a chaotic aspect as the two retiring managers gloomily folded files, selected mementos, disputed ownership of souvenirs, and gave orders for the disposition of furniture to a small army of movers, who paraded in and out, carrying items of every description. In the confusion, they did not appear to regard my intrusion as out of the ordinary.

Outside the grimy windows, three floors down, the steam shovels and jackhammers were at work in a light drizzle on the Rue Scribe underground line, their faint cacophony adding to the dissonance within.

"The end of an era—the Poligny-Debienne era," observed Poligny.

"The Debienne-Poligny era," corrected his alter ego, accompanying this amendment with a portentous sigh.

"I should like to speak with Mademoiselle Christine Daaé," I interrupted.

"Not here," said Poligny, studying a pile of documents before handing them over to Debienne, who glanced at them briefly before handing them back.

"We did some good work," stated Debienne, looking at a poster on the wall.

"Very good work."

"Where might I find her?"

For the first time, they regarded me.

"I do not understand why you are making this request, Monsieur . . ."

"Sigerson," I reminded them. "I am, as you will recall, a friend of Mademoiselle Adler's."

"Monsieur Sigerson," said Poligny, "you will forgive us, but your association with Mademoiselle Adler, while doubtless impressive, does not constitute a *passe-partout.*"

"I am afraid you will have to do better than that," added Debienne, crunching a pile of papers and tossing them into the rubbish. I took a breath.

"Very well, gentlemen, you compel me to tell you the truth."

"Aha," said Poligny, without paying the slightest attention.

"I am here at the instigation of Scotland Yard," I told them, assuming my best Etonian accent.

They both ceased their labors at once and looked at me.

"What?"

"At the request of Monsieur Mifroid of the Paris prefecture," I added, switching back to French, "I have been installed as a mem-

ber of the orchestra in order that I may look into the death of Joseph Buquet."

I prayed, as I said this, that the two men were sufficiently distracted by their own affairs that they would not recollect that I had actually begun my employment in the orchestra *before* Buquet was killed, in which case I might find myself a suspect.

"Scotland Yard?" echoed Debienne. A tic or spasm had begun at his right eye, and he pulled at it with his hand. "Why should the prefecture need an Englishman to help investigate Buquet's death?"

"They did not need an Englishman," I explained, affecting a slight air of impatience, "they needed a policeman who could play the violin." I had their complete attention now.

"Leroux always said you were no Norwegian," Poligny suddenly recalled. "Your name?"

I nearly choked as I said it, Watson, but I had no makeup to disguise me, only my wits. May God forgive me.

"Inspector Lestrade.* I carry no identification with me, for obvious reasons," I continued somewhat hastily, "but Mademoiselle Adler will confirm my identity, I am certain."

The two men subsided into the chairs behind their desks.

"Scotland Yard," they repeated.

"The prefecture regards this matter as most serious, gentlemen. Might I trouble you for some privacy?"

Poligny hesitated, then addressed the movers.

"Get out," said he. "We will send for you." The movers shrugged and departed, indifferent to the change of plans. I sensed them contemplating the prospect of a little *apéritif.*

---

*Of all the Scotland Yarders, Holmes probably regarded Lestrade as the most incompetent.

"Now then," I resumed, when Debienne had closed the door on the last of them, "what can you tell me about the Ghost?"

They exchanged wary looks.

"Show him the contract," Poligny instructed Debienne.

With another sigh, Debienne produced a key from his pocket with which he opened a large safe in a corner of the room. He rummaged amongst the mess there, withdrawing, at length, several sheets of paper, which he handed me, his eyelid twitching like an epileptic semaphore.

"These are the conditions of the Opéra lease," he explained, covering his eye with his hand. "Most of the clauses are standard."

"So I see," I remarked, scanning the document.

"We draw your attention, however, to the three conditions which follow upon clause sixty-seven."

I flipped through the pages rapidly and came upon the conditions, scrawled in an elegant hand, distinguishing them from the typescript which characterized the bulk of the contract.

"These addenda were found by us *in the safe,* shortly after the beginning of our tenure," Poligny remarked, propping his chin on one elbow and watching me unhappily as I read them. "We have the only key," he added, as if I could not understand his implication.

"These then are the conditions stipulated by the Ghost?"

"Precisely."

The conditions were these:

   I.   Box five Grand Tier shall always be reserved for the exclusive use of the Ghost.

  II.   The Ghost may from time to time demand substitutions in the cast of certain performances. These substitutions are to be carried out without question or demur.

III. The Ghost shall receive a cash disbursement on the first of
every month, consisting of 20,000 francs. Should the management for any reason delay for more than a fortnight of
any month the payment of the Ghost's allowance (which
shall total 240,000 francs a year), the Ghost shall not be held
responsible for the consequences.

I looked up.

"You have adhered to these conditions?"

"To the letter," Debienne answered. "We found it safer to do
so."

"It is curious that the Ghost demands money," I suggested.

"Curiosity killed the cat," responded Poligny.

"At any rate, we now know whence Madame Giry receives her
three francs tip," I murmured, more to myself than to them. "And
how is the money transferred?"

"Madame Giry leaves it in an envelope in his box on the first
of each month. We appropriate the funds from the maintenance
budget."

"The fools!" Debienne burst forth suddenly, the spasm now
wildly out of control. "They have no idea what they are doing!" He
ran an agitated hand through his thinning hair.

"To whom do you refer?"

"Why, to Moncharmin and Richard, the new directors!"
shouted Poligny, as if he were addressing an idiot. "They are court-
ing disaster!"

"How so?" Again the hapless men exchanged glances.

"They do not believe in the existence of the Ghost," Debienne
complained, passing a hand over his haggard brow. "They appear
to think the whole idea is some sort of elaborate practical joke on
our part and they have made plain that they want none of it."

"A joke," echoed Poligny with a doleful laugh.

"Indeed?"

"Indeed. They have said they will not honor the addenda in the contract. They will not pay his money, they will not change the casts, and worst of all, they will sell box five!"

"Beginning tonight!" added Poligny, shaking his head. "They plan to occupy it themselves! They have dismissed Madame Giry," he went on, as if relating news of sacrilege, "and threatened some sort of replacement!"

"Worse," Debienne pursued, "they have insisted that La Sorelli sing tonight. *Mon Dieu,*"he muttered, in a terrified whisper.

"This, too, is a violation?" I inquired.

"We explained most carefully that the Ghost has demanded Christine Daaé sing the role of Marguerite this evening in *Faust.* They laughed at us," concluded Poligny. I could not help noticing that the two men invariably took turns speaking.

"How did the Ghost convey his desire that Mademoiselle Daaé sing tonight?"

"He talks to us."

"Directly?"

"As directly as we speak to you now, Inspector. We hear his voice here in the office."

"Through the ether," supplied Debienne, anticipating my next question. "He talks anywhere and everywhere in the building. And he hears everything that is said."

"That is suggestive."

"I don't know what you mean."

"It is not important that you should," I informed them, for indeed they were imminently to be quit of the entire business. "At what time did the Ghost inform you of his intended alteration of this evening's cast?"

"Ten o'clock this morning, just after I had come into this office," Poligny answered without hesitation. "I begged them to listen to reason," he pointed out to Debienne.

"Begged and begged again," the other confirmed. I rose.

"Gentlemen, I must reiterate my first request." They favored me with identical blank expressions. "Where can I find Mademoiselle Daaé?"

"She lives with her invalid grandmother."

"I understood her to be an orphan."

"Not really her grandmother, but an elderly widow she honors with the name who has rooms in the Rue Gaspard. She calls herself Mother Valerius, I believe."

"Thank you." I started for the door, and they saw me hesitate.

"Yes?"

"I was simply curious. What becomes of managers such as yourselves when your tenure is concluded at a place such as this?"

They cast brief glances at one another.

"Sir," explained Debienne, drawing himself up to his full height, "you have the honor of addressing the new directors of the Tabor Opera House of Leadville, Colorado."

"Forgive me, messieurs, for trespassing on your valuable time."

7

THE ANGEL

*Y*ou will recall, Watson, that in the business of the Dartmoor Horror, which you were pleased to set down and publish as *The Hound of the Baskervilles,* I explained to you that I knew from the first we were dealing with no spectral dog. From the moment a very real boot was stolen from Sir Henry Baskerville at the Northumberland Hotel, I was in not the slightest doubt. No ghostly hound had need of an earthly scent to help him track his prey.

And no Ghost needed twenty thousand francs per month.

I was now of the opinion that the so-called Ghost and Buquet's murderer were one and the same, very likely an individual who was employed by the Opéra and who commanded a working knowledge of its complex innards. He had developed a passionate regard for Mademoiselle Daaé, an attraction that would likely prove fatal to any and all rivals in contention for her affections. It therefore seemed prudent, before matters had gone any further, to interview

the young woman over whose welfare I had been deputized to stand guard. I would attempt to learn what she knew of her invisible suitor in the hopes that such knowledge would assist me to lay him by the heels before any more damage was done.

Mother Valerius's rooms on the Rue Gaspard were simple enough, but clean. There was a maid, but it was the object of my curiosity herself who answered my knock. She wore an attractive dark blue dressing gown with a touch of white at the wrists and throat. Close to, Christine Daaé was even more lovely than I had been able to determine from my seat in the stalls during the performance of *Le Prophète*. Her hair was a rich blond, at present worn in plaits, framing a heart-shaped face with unclouded brow and wide-set grey eyes that danced with the liveliness of the eighteen-year-old she was. Her nose was small but straight, her chin strong just short of obstinacy, and her skin had a youthful glow, a trifle paler than her rosebud lips. I daresay she was very much the sort of creature who would have appealed to you, Watson, in palmier days. She had, as I knew, no shortage of admirers, and looking upon her now, I could readily comprehend the extremes to which her beauty might lead them.

"Monsieur Sigerson, come in!"

My presence seemed to afford her no particular astonishment. When I inquired as to the reason for this, she smiled.

"But I have heard all about you from Irene! She has told me I may trust in you as in herself, and I believe all she says. She had a sort of premonition you might call upon me." Failing to notice my inward sigh of relief and gratitude to the farsighted Miss Adler, the young woman had turned to present me to her invalid guardian, the cheerful Mother Valerius, who sat up in a heavily quilted four-poster bed and greeted me gaily.

"*Chérie,* fetch Monsieur Sigerson some tea!"

"But of course, *grandmaman!*" said the girl and skipped from the room before I could object.

"She is a good girl," the old woman said, nodding in the direction of the door.

"How did you come to know her?" I asked.

"Her father, poor man, rented rooms from me till the day he was taken."

"Taken?"

She raised her eyes heavenward.

"A lovely man, a veritable saint, and how he adored his child!"

"I understand he was her only teacher of music."

"As you can hear, monsieur, she never needed another."

By and by the girl came back with tea things neatly assembled on a tray.

"Take your caller into the sitting room, child," instructed Mother Valerius. "You have no need to entertain me."

Christine protested but at length gave way to the gentle but persistent commands of her guardian.

"Yes, Irene told me you would come," she repeated, pouring the brew into my cup and handing it to me. "How thoughtful of her to send you as my protector, knowing she must soon leave for Amsterdam. I thought perhaps you would prove to be my second angel," she added with a mischievous smile.

"Your second? Do you regard Mademoiselle Adler as your first?"

"Oh, no." She could hardly stifle a giggle. "I adore Mademoiselle Adler and she is many things, but she would never claim to be an angel."

Silently I agreed with her.

"Do you know anything of the Opéra Ghost?" I began. To my astonishment, she laughed heartily. "There is no Opéra Ghost."

"No? But—"

"*That* is my first angel!"

She could not have astounded me more had she taken flight, which in her excitement she threatened to do.

"The Ghost is no ghost, but an angel?"

"I will tell you," she said simply, but with an ecstatic air that caused me faint unease. "I am dying to tell you! When my father taught me singing, he often told me about the Angel of Music."

"The Angel of Music?"

"My father was a most religious man, monsieur, and he raised me to love the saints! When he listened to my voice he said it was so wonderful that if I heeded my studies and worked very hard, perhaps one day I should be visited by the Angel of Music, whose inspiration would complete my education. Alas, that he never lived to see that day," she concluded with a sigh.

Under cover of swallowing some of my tea, I examined the girl closely. There was not an ounce of guile in her face, nor any intimation of duplicity in her clear grey eyes. On the contrary, I began to see what Irene Adler had meant when she referred to the possibility that Christine Daaé was so simple as to be almost simpleminded. It was clear from the crucifix on the wall and the demureness of her expression that deception was quite beyond her.

"And the angel came to you at last?"

She nodded eagerly, bursting to share her secret with someone.

"In my dressing room, three months ago! Oh, he has the loveliest voice imaginable, and he is an excellent teacher!" she added, as though this were the final proof of his identity.

"He teaches you?" Irene Adler's impression had proved no fancy.

"Daily. He is very strict, but very gentle. When he instructs me,

it is as if he reads my mind, for he knows my very thoughts and dreams! And when I sing afterwards, it is as if another being inhabited my voice, my very soul.''

I remembered Leroux's remark about the unevenness of Christine's singing and the consensus that his observation was an accurate assessment. "Does he sing himself?"

"Oh, monsieur, he has the most beautiful voice! Only that voice can express the inexpressible longing that is in every human breast, the longing to be understood, to be loved. And he is a composer, as well!'' she went on, clapping her hands with enthusiasm.

"A composer?"

"He works daily on his opera and tells me all about it. *Don Juan Triumphant,* he calls it, and he promises that when it is finished he will take me to hear it performed!" Her eyes glistened at the prospect.

Here was a chilling thought.

"He composes at the organ?"

"How did you know?"

"Idle speculation, I assure you. I gather the angel had little use for Joseph Buquet," I hazarded.

She nodded, lowering her head. "But he did not harm him," she declared emphatically. "It was Raoul who threw poor Joseph out of my dressing room. He is very jealous, however," she amended in a thoughtful tone.

"The Vicomte?"

"My angel."

"For you?"

"He wishes me to save myself."

"For himself?"

"For my music," she corrected with a startled look. It was clear that no one had told her about the missing hangman's rope.

"How would you describe Buquet during the altercation with the Vicomte?" I wondered. She gnawed a finger in concentration.

"He was upset."

"Can you be more precise? Was he frightened? Angry?"

"Very angry."

"When he left your dressing room, you did not set him down as a man about to do away with himself?"

I could see the idea did not sit well with her.

"It all happened so quickly, monsieur."

Seeing this line of questioning to be rather a dead end, I chose to backtrack.

"I take it the Ghost has no love for the poor Vicomte de Chagny, either."

She paled at this, and her hand fluttered involuntarily to her throat.

"As you love God, monsieur, you must keep Raoul away from me!"

"Why?"

"Because . . . I have told you . . . my angel expects . . . he insists that I save my voice for my art."

"Are you quite certain that is all he wishes you to save?"

She favored me with a blank expression, which was succeeded in turn by a worried frown.

"I must not anger him," she said urgently, "or he will take away my voice!"

"Nonsense."

"And he may do Raoul a mischief!"

"Angels do not usually harm people," I did not scruple to point out to her.

"Have you never heard of avenging angels?" she countered, grasping my hand in hers and pressing it passionately. "Please make him stay away! I love him"—here she lowered her voice and

cast an anxious glance around the room as if fearful of being over-heard—"but he must stay away!"

"The young man loves you, and he cannot understand why—"

"Please!" Her voice was now constricted by fear. "I beg of you!"

"And have you no fears for yourself from the avenging angel?"

She looked at me in astonishment, blinking her eyes, then pointed at herself, pressing an index finger to her breast.

"Me? Oh, he would never harm me—never for all the world! He loves me!"

Seeing how agitated she had become, I resolved to change the subject. I patted her hand and gently pried it lose from its grip on my wrist, then sipped some more tea.

"I understand *Faust* is to be given this evening."

"Yes. *Faust.*"

"Are you disappointed not to be singing Marguerite?"

"Oh, but I shall be singing."

"I see Carlotta Sorelli listed on the programme." She laughed, a high-spirited, girlish laugh, taking me by the shoulders and inviting me to share her mirth.

"I know that she is listed, but that is just his way! He loves to tease and provoke me! He has promised I am to sing tonight, and I never doubt him. He has sworn that my performance this evening will bring down the house. And when he promises a thing I may depend on it!"

Before I could respond to this intelligence, the clock above the mantel chimed three in discreet tones.

"Heavens," she exclaimed, "I must take my nap. The angel insists I get my rest before a performance. Will you forgive me?"

"Of course."

It was as well, for I had no notion of how to continue this grotesque conversation. It was evident to me the girl's mental state was extremely delicate, and I knew better from recent experience than to tamper with the fragile mechanisms and wellsprings of a human heart in such a precarious condition.

I rose and took my leave, asking that my thanks be conveyed to Mother Valerius.

"Oh, I shall thank her, as I thank Mademoiselle Adler for sending you to me. I feel quite confident now that all will be well!" And rising briefly on tiptoe, she planted an innocent kiss on my cheek.

"One last question, if I may, mademoiselle."

She hesitated, smiling in the half-open doorway.

"Does this—does your angel have a name?"

"But of course. He is called Nobody."

"Nobody?" It was impossible to suppress the inflection of surprise in my voice, and I could see it startled her.

"Is something wrong?"

"Not at all. Do you speak English, mademoiselle?"

"Not a word. Why?"

"Mere curiosity. Good day."

8

SECOND BLOOD

I stood in the Rue Gaspard, Watson, midday Parisian traffic swirling and hurtling about me, horses clip-clopping everywhere, and realized that it was a very pretty problem. It was in fact quite a three-pipe problem—my only difficulty was that I had not three pipes' time in which to resolve it. In less than six hours the curtain was due to rise on *Faust*.

Consider my position. I knew that Messieurs Moncharmin and Richard were determined to flout all three clauses in the Ghost's contract.

I strongly suspected the Ghost or the angel or Nobody or whatever name one gave him of being responsible for the death of Joseph Buquet.

I knew also he had sworn Christine Daaé would sing this night, this Nobody.

Poor, credulous, highly strung, docile, and devout Christine,

who could no more imagine evil than she could sing off-key, in the thrall of a rogue who meddled with her feeble intellect and preyed on her parochial innocence. And this fellow, Watson, deemed her his exclusive property, by right of his personal *droit du seigneur.*

All of these things pointed strongly to some mischief, yet the more I considered the matter, the more helpless I understood myself to be.

How could I alone prevent matters from unfolding as the phantom wished?

And if I could not succeed alone (as seemed probable), where could I go with my suspicions and what kind of assistance was I seeking?

Go the police, I hear you say. Good old Watson, you always march the straightest course. Go to the police and tell them what? That I suspect? That I feel? That I fear? I hadn't a shred of proof, my boy, and my intimations of disaster were founded upon trifles. Such trifles, as you know, I regard as paramount in forging my chain of logic, but they do not of themselves constitute evidence. Were I dull as Lestrade himself or keen as Hopkins I would have dismissed the matter out of hand.*

And why should they listen to me, in any event, a mere violinist?

Tell them who you are! I hear you exclaim. Forgo your incognito!

You may be sure that I considered revealing my true identity, Watson. Human lives were quite possibly at stake, and these considerations must finally transcend my own motives for concealment. But in the next instant it readily became apparent that such a reve-

*One assumes Holmes is here referring to Inspector Stanley Hopkins of Scotland Yard, whom he did not encounter until 1895. Nevertheless, narrating these events in 1912, Holmes was doubtless using Hopkins as an example of the best that the Yard had to offer.

lation was likely to harm my case, rather than enhance it. There was even the distinct likelihood that it might result in my incarceration at a time when liberty would be most precious to me. In a word, how could I claim to be Sherlock Holmes when all the world, including the Paris press, had reported him dead? Might not such a claim cast doubt on whatever it was I wanted the police to hear? Upon my very sanity? Might it not lead to my detention or arrest as a potentially dangerous fellow?

No, the police were out of the question. Even were they to pay me heed, what would be the result? Hundreds of officers milling about the Opéra, distracting the audience? These might well put my adversary off, causing him to cancel his plans entirely, in which case the police would certainly think me mad and I should again have placed myself in jeopardy.

My best course seemed rather to approach Moncharmin and Richard. I would attempt to sway these two gentlemen from the implementation of their new policies before they had cause to regret them.

Here again, difficulties lay in my way.

I knew both gentlemen to be at a government luncheon, celebrating the inauguration of their tenure, and I was due for a special rehearsal called for two in the afternoon. I could not risk forfeiting my position by failing to attend. Dismissal from the Opéra was the last thing I could afford at present. All I could hope was to corner the new managers following the rehearsal and before the evening's performance, which was cutting matters rather too fine for my taste, but I saw no way around my dilemma. In the meantime, I would pay a call on the Vicomte and pass on Christine Daaé's words of warning. I was uncertain whether my mandate to protect Mademoiselle Daaé included playing Cupid by relaying reassurances to her lover, but he at least might listen to what I had to say. I had no wish to see him suffer the same fate as Joseph Buquet.

At the Avenue Kléber, Henri, the retainer, answered the bell and endeavored to put me off.

"I am under strict instructions to admit no one," said he firmly, like his master proposing to bar the door in my face. This time, however, my foot intercepted it on the jamb.

"It is a matter of utmost gravity that I speak with the Vicomte at once," I told him. "Should you forbid me entry, I will have no alternative than to create a disturbance."

Henri, as I have noted, was not a young man, and the prospect of what I might do, with one foot literally in the door, decided him.

I found the de Chagny brothers in the library, which seemed rather too full of unread volumes. I was not surprised to see the Vicomte nursing a headache with cups of black coffee. Evidently he had only just risen. Monsieur le Comte, I gathered, was in the middle of a lecture, and knit his brows darkly at the sight of me.

"I hope you will forgive my intrusion," I began, "and forgive your servant, who admitted me rather than cause a scene."

"Who are you and what do you want?" demanded the Comte in a haughty tone. On another occasion, Watson, I should have liked to teach him manners, but for the present, I stuck to my errand.

"I am a friend of your brother's and I bear him a message from Mademoiselle Daaé."

The little Vicomte looked up at this, hope flooding his puffy features, but the Comte, his own countenance suffused with anger, spoke first.

"The Vicomte has no plans for any further communication with the person to whom you refer," he informed me in the same condescending tone. "We shall shortly be leaving the city for a bit of shooting at our chateau in Normandy."

"Philippe," interposed the young man, feebly looking up, but

the other's hand lay forcefully upon his shoulder and he said no more.

"I am here to tell you that is exactly what the young woman desires," said I, speaking directly to the Vicomte as if his brother did not exist. "She tells you that she loves you—"

"That will *do!*" roared the Comte, advancing on me in a threatening manner. He was a large man and the prospect of trouncing him made my mouth fairly water.*

"She loves me!" echoed the happy youth, rising unsteadily to his feet.

"—but that it would be best for you not to see her at present," I went on, quite unconcerned, "until this business is finished. You may rest easy now," said I, addressing the Comte. "I am leaving."

The little Vicomte remained uncertainly on his feet and proffered me a tentative wave behind his brother's back.

I was barely in my chair when the rehearsal began. One of the droller aspects of operatic performance is the incessant substitutions of singers, usually on short notice. A singer's vocal apparatus being such a susceptible mechanism, the most delicate deviation can be responsible for its collapse. I once attended a performance of *Bohème* at Covent Garden in which each member of the quartet of lovers was replaced, in each of the successive four acts, so that by the conclusion of the piece, none of the original singers was left. Rodolpho was indisposed following the first act; Musetta, following the second; Mimi dropped out during the third; and Marcello was not himself in the fourth. By the time of the opera's finale, four complete strangers professed their undying passion for one another.

---

*Holmes's abilities as a boxer, swordsman, singlestick player, and baritsu expert are too well known to need description here.

The present rehearsal was called for two instead of ten in order that Gerhardt Huxtable, replacing the overtaxed Jean de Rezske (who would be singing in *Faust* this evening), could learn the role of Don José in our production of *Carmen*. Irene Adler, still performing the eponymous role, engaged to help Huxtable through this start-and-stop affair, teaching him the stage moves called "blocking."

I confess my mind was not occupied by the music as the afternoon drifted by. The complaints of the chorus, who objected to smoking in Act I, I had heard before. I was too concerned by the need to speak to the directors and make my case before another incident occurred to pay much attention to Act II. Time, as I have said, conspired against me on this occasion. Late in Act III, as the muscular Huxtable engaged in his knife fight with Escamillo, his matador rival for the favors of Carmen, I found myself thinking about the Ghost—Nobody, as Christine Daaé had called him—and his little tricks. It was evident that his infatuation with the young soprano had assumed such proportions that anyone who sought her favors or her friendship was at risk. We had already been treated to the fate of poor Buquet, and the girl herself was in a frenzy of alarm for her young lover.

We were well into the fourth act of our *répétition* when another thought struck me: Irene Adler had adopted Christine Daaé— taken her under her wing, as she had phrased it. In fact, now that I turned the matter over in my mind, Irene Adler had done much more; she had interested herself in Christine Daaé's affairs to the extent that she had engaged the services of a detective. While my mind rejected the idea of the Ghost's being omniscient, I suddenly found myself speculating as to whether his jealousy was limited to the male sex. If, as I suspected, his mental condition made no such distinctions, then Miss Adler was herself in danger—the more so as she was at present within the creature's domain.

As Carmen swore her eternal detestation of the cast-off Don José (the redoubtable and energetic Huxtable, who appeared positively to relish the physical aspects of his degradation, wallowing in humbled virility), and as the offstage chorus rejoiced at Escamillo's triumph, I found my mind racing over the possibilities. With the exception of Buquet's apparent suicide, the Ghost's usual repertoire favored pranks and accidents.

Bizet, with a fondness for irony, had contrived that the finale of his opera depicted a real murder outside a bullfight arena, watched by a real audience, whilst simultaneously "within" the arena—that is to say, offstage—an unseen matador (he invented the word *toreador* because he needed the additional syllable) skewered an unseen bull before an unseen mob. It was the sort of thing that was bound to appeal to Nobody's taste for the sensational and the bizarre.

Overhead, the quarrel between Carmen and José grew more desperate. Any moment now, José would draw his knife and gut her like a mackerel, finishing the opera by crying out her name.

His knife.

In a flash I had leapt from my chair and bolted through the door of the pit, racing for the ladder and charging upwards to the stage. I had no time to glance about me, only to rush out from the wings and fling myself upon Miss Adler, interposing my body between her own and the animated knife thrust of the tenor, to the consternation of all and sundry as we toppled to the floor.

"Sherlock!"

Can you imagine the effect of hearing that name on her lips, Watson? A jolt went through my body like an electric current, even as I clapped a hand over the mouth that uttered it.

"Are you all right? Dear God, say you are not harmed!" I cried, staring down at her waxen features.

The knife was of the sort manufactured exclusively for use in

theatrical performance, the blade cunningly designed to retract into its handle the moment it encountered any form of resistance, such as a body. The victim, by clutching the handle tightly against himself, might create the impression of impalement. When he or another actor "pulled" smartly at the handle, the blade, prompted by an inner spring, would snap back as the knife was "removed" from the "wound."

In the present instance, however, the blade had unaccountably stuck, refusing to vanish into its hidden receptacle. Miss Adler had been grazed by its point, but, thanks to my unorthodox intercession, no serious damage was done.

"It worked perfectly during the knife fight in Act III," Escamillo pointed out.

"I swear, Monsieur Mercier," shouted the prop master, "no one has been near my prop table! No one!"

"Of course not, Léonard. It was an accident," Mercier, the stage manager, declared, fiddling with the blade and freeing it from its constraint.

"What was that she cried out?" someone demanded. "It sounded like—"

"She asked if someone would please fetch a glass of water," I interpreted curtly. In short order the water appeared. With some effort, I helped Miss Adler to sit up. She was still deathly pale, her features stamped with an alarm I had never yet beheld on them.

"Can you drink this?" I asked gently. She nodded and swallowed.

"You have saved my life," said she, taking several deep breaths.

"If that is true, I have justified my own existence."

She favored me with the briefest of glances and then allowed me to help her to her feet. I was suddenly aware that I was the object of some curiosity. At the point when it would have become awkward

for me, however, attention was diverted from my prescience by the sudden collapse of the heroic Gerhardt Huxtable, who had fainted dead away at the sight of Miss Adler's scratch.

Leroux harrumphed and said something from the pit about that being all for today's rehearsal.

"How did you know there was something wrong with the knife?" Bela demanded of me as we put away our instruments.

"Merely a sixth sense, Bela."

"But—" Ponelle began.

"You must excuse me," I interrupted him. "I am late for an urgent appointment."

IT WAS CLOSE TO SIX before I was admitted into the presence of the new managing directors of the Opéra. Moncharmin, it must be said at once, *looked* like a managing director, being tall and wearing distinguished side-whiskers and a well-waxed imperial of the same ivory hue, in defiant memory of the late Emperor. He knew nothing of music and could not tell one note from another. Ponelle had been no more than just when he called opera managers idiots. Richard, on the contrary, resembled the accountant he doubtless was, but claimed some familiarity with the repertoire.

The offices of the new directors seemed to be in no less a state of chaos than when they had been occupied by their predecessors. The two gentlemen, already in evening dress, were energetically supervising a phalanx of frenzied secretaries regarding the distribution of ticket passes for the Opéra Masked Ball, two days hence, an annual event in Paris of the most supreme social significance.

"And all the passes are not delivered yet!" cried Moncharmin.

"And a good thing, too," retorted Richard querulously, "considering to whom some of them are addressed! They must have been mad," he added, referring, I presumed, to Debienne and

Poligny and holding up an envelope as if it were contaminated by some disease. "This is intended for that Jew banker de Reinach."

"What's wrong with de Reinach?" demanded Moncharmin, pawing through another pile of envelopes. "He has plenty of money."

"Don't you read the papers? He is implicated in the Panama debacle!"*

Moncharmin straightened up at this.

"You don't say. Cross him off, then."

"Gentlemen," I said, coughing to remind them of my presence.

"Oh, yes, what is it, Sigerson?"

"I have come to deliver a warning. From the Ghost," I added, hoping to gain their attention.

"Not again. My dear man, we have already been warned. We have indeed been subject to a surfeit of warnings."

Seeing the surprise on my face, Richard shrugged and produced a note, written in a familiar hand on familiar paper. It ran:

So you propose to break the terms of our contract? Be warned, for I give no quarter.

It was unsigned.

"We found it in our offices this morning," Richard explained.

"This is in the same handwriting and on the same paper as the addenda," I pointed out.

"So it is," Moncharmin allowed.

*Baron Jacques de Reinach was one of the earliest backers of Ferdinand de Lesseps' French scheme to build a canal across the Isthmus of Panama. That effort collapsed after ten years in the largest financial scandal of the nineteenth century, while Holmes was in Paris. De Reinach subsequently committed suicide.

"Does this suggest nothing to either of you?"

"Only that we continue to be victims of a practical joke which has gone on quite long enough," Richard stated flatly.

"Gentlemen, there is no joke and no Ghost," I began. Nevertheless I earnestly enjoined them not to flout the conditions of the addenda. They heard me out in impatient silence as I put before them what I knew. I told them in the firmest language at my command that the Ghost, whatever his true name or identity, was not to be trifled with, that lives were at risk. I urged them to engage Madame Giry once more and to abandon their plans to occupy box five. Above all, I pleaded with them to allow Christine Daaé to sing Marguerite this night. The issue of the money I felt could wait.

"Change the cast?" Moncharmin asked, looking incredulous. Of all I had said, only this last appeared to penetrate his cerebellum.

"Such changes occur all the time," I reminded him.

"But for a ghost—!"

"It is no ghost but a man, someone I suspect of being in the employ of the Opéra itself, a man with a grudge and a dangerous temper."

I now relayed to them the latest prank of the Ghost and its near consequences.

"Who did you say you were?" Moncharmin demanded with a puzzled air.

"He's the policeman who plays the violin," Richard reminded him. "You recall Poligny telling us. The prefecture has got him looking into the business of the dead scene-shifter," he added when Moncharmin seemed still at a loss.

To my astonishment, the latter burst out laughing.

"My friend," said Moncharmin, clapping a hand about my shoulder, "you have played your part quite well."

"My part?"

"Of course! We would never have taken you for a policeman, you are such a good violinist!" He laughed, pleased with his own wit.

"But really," he added, "as you can see, we are terribly busy. "Have you included the Marquis de Saint-Evremonde?"* he asked Richard, returning to the task uppermost in his mind.

"Yes, the commissionaire has left already."

"I must assure you, gentlemen, this is no joke. One man is already dead and no less a personage than Mademoiselle Irene Adler was almost killed one hour ago in this building by a prop knife which failed to retract."

"Yes, we've heard all about the knife accident," Richard informed me. "But some chap got there just in time. All's well that ends well, I always say."

"The prop master will be given the sack, of course," added the other.

"You cannot possibly believe this was truly an accident," I implored. "Gentlemen, I beg of you—before it is too late!"

"Whatever it is, then, we have had quite enough of it. I can assure you the Opéra will not continue to be run in the slapdash fashion of our predecessors," Moncharmin informed me in a friendly but firm tone. "We appreciate your attempt at levity, *mon ami,* but while this sort of rude frontier humor may suffice in Leadville"—he fairly gagged on the word—"it will no longer be tolerated in Paris. Meantime, if you will pardon us, we have much to do before this evening and we are certain there are other claims upon your own valuable time."

"You absolutely refuse to consider any of my urgent appeals?"

---

*This aristocratic family was hunted to the brink of extinction during the Terror (1793), but survived in an offshoot who called himself Darnay. One of Darnay's descendants (he married the daughter of a Bastille prisoner and produced children by her) evidently reassumed the family name and title.

They looked at each other, now betraying faint traces of irritation.

"Please thank Messieurs Debienne and Poligny for their persistence," said Richard, escorting me to the door, "but there comes a time when every joke wears out its welcome."

"You are determined, then, to occupy box five this evening?"

"Quite determined."

"Then at least allow me to share the box."

"What?"

"Out of the question." Moncharmin bristled with indignation at my presumption. "Your musical duties—"

"Are superseded by my responsibilities as a police officer," I countered smoothly. "Besides which, I offer to pay for my seat."

This caused him to hesitate. I glanced from one to the other with the most sympathetic expression I could summon.

Richard shrugged.

"As you like, Sigerson. But stay well in the shadows."

"Yes, keep in the shadows," Moncharmin echoed this order happily. "After all, this is our night."

9

THE ANGEL'S WORK

Time was now so short that I was unable even to ask after Irene Adler, who I knew had been escorted to her hotel. A telephone call was all I could manage, and the desk clerk assured me that he had personally seen her to her suite. There was nothing else I could accomplish on that front. More pressing matters demanded my best efforts.

Before changing into my own evening dress, I resolved one last futile attempt.

"Where can I find a set of plans for the Opéra?" I asked old Jérôme at the stage door.

"The next tour leaves in fifteen minutes," he said, without looking up or removing from his mouth the stub of a pipe which was clenched between his three remaining teeth.

"What tour?"

"Exactly!" he snarled. "You think this is the bloody Eiffel Tower? Plans!" he snorted and returned to his paper.

Mercier, the stage manager, was slightly more informative.

"There's no complete set in the building," he said, shrugging as he considered my request. "At least nothing that goes below cellar four—that's the stables. Each department knows its own location and what it requires." He shrugged again, smoothing a stubborn cowlick at the back of his head. "I suppose you could go to the City Planning Commission in the Rue de Varenne, though I doubt it's open now. Why do you want them?"

There was nothing for it but to descend without any plans into the labyrinth in search of this latter-day Minotaur. Following the example of Theseus, I procured a ball of green yarn from the wardrobe department and below level two commenced unspooling it in my wake as I twisted along corridors and through doorways.

What was I trying to achieve? I knew better than to anticipate discovering the creature itself; rather I was desperate to unearth some clue as to his *modus operandi*—for it was clear he had the run of the place—and I would settle for anything that would subsequently enable me to flush him from his cover.

After several endless tunnels, I came upon the hard dirt circular path the horses used and followed it downwards till it led me to the Opéra stables. To this point I had encountered no one, but at the stables the hostlers were engaged in a furious debate.

"What are you doing down here?" one of them demanded, approaching me with a truculent swagger.

"It's all right, it's Sigerson," said my friend Jacques. "It wasn't him, for heaven's sake."

"What has happened?" I had to pose the question several times before one of them would answer.

"You know César?"

"The beautiful white gelding from *Mondego*?"

"He's been stolen!"

"You don't say. When?"

"Just now—that is to say, within the past twelve hours. There are only fourteen horses in the stables at present—were, I should say, for César's disappeared and there'll be hell to pay."

"They'll sack the lot of us, that's what," prophesied the outspoken groom who had approached me earlier.

"I take it there is no way he could have wandered off?"

"Wandered where? He could only go up, monsieur, and that leads to the stage."

"What about down?"

They shook their heads.

"See for yourself, monsieur. There's an iron gate that is locked always, and this separates the rest of the building from the lake. No one I know of possesses the key. It hasn't been opened for some time, as you can see by the lock, which has frozen."

The gate to which he had conducted me entirely filled an archway eighteen feet in height, ending flush with the ceiling and scraping along the stone floor so that no human, much less a horse, could pass through. The lock had not been tampered with in years.

"Are the stables unmanned at night?"

"The stables are never unmanned. There are always at least two of us on duty. Is there something we can do for you, monsieur? We are rather busy just at present . . ."

"I understand." Everybody was too busy for me this fateful day. I turned to retrace my steps, then halted. "Tell me, do you ever hear sounds?"

"Sounds like what?" asked honest Jacques.

"Music, for example."

"Oh, all the time. The organist."

"The organist."

"He practices constantly, the music floats down. And sometimes we hear him singing—a fine rich baritone."

I found myself wondering if the music didn't float *up*.

"I see. Thank you. I shall certainly keep an eye out for César."

"Lot of good that will do," I heard one of them mutter as I began following my trail of yarn up the dirt path towards the theatre, rewinding it as I walked.

When I reached level two, I rounded a corner and stopped dead.

The yarn had been severed. The rest of my green trail was nowhere to be seen. I had a fair idea of where I was; cutting it had not been designed to prevent my returning, only to manifest the presence of my unseen adversary. He specialized in the most ominous calling cards.

And now I heard again the faint sound of disembodied laughter.

I changed my apparel and took my seat as instructed, behind Moncharmin and Richard, at the rear of box five. I had a clear view of the stage as the new managers bowed and preened before the audience, enjoying to the fullest their debut. Nothing could allay my sense of foreboding. I had prowled backstage beforehand and discovered naught amiss. I had terrified poor Léonard into never taking his eyes from the prop table for the next four hours. The *corps de ballet* was happily nattering like a gaggle of geese, the chorus pulling on tights and adjusting wigs, La Sorelli vocalizing in her dressing room.

I made bold to inquire if she had heard any rumors.

"Bah. I even get the threatening letter."

"May I see it?"

"I throw it away," she said contemptuously. "I get them all the

time," she added. " 'Sorelli, do not sing tonight! You have the frog in the throat!' Bah!" She laughed again. "This is a plot by the claque. It was the same at La Scala. La Sorelli never have the frog."

"Whose claque?"

"Why, that slut La Daaé, of course. They think to make her career over my dead body!" Her laughs were like the barks of a small dog, but she was not to be intimidated. Christine Daaé was a rival, and threats or no threats, Sorelli intended to perform.

"You look like a man with something on his mind," Ponelle had commented, watching me surveying the house from the wings before he went into the pit.

"Very likely," was all he got out of me. I told him to make my excuses to Leroux. His eyes widened at this, but he left without pressing me for an explanation.

From my vantage point between Moncharmin and Richard I spied a small woman in row M whose clothes did not look as though they belonged to her and who was casting amazed glances about the auditorium, twisting her head in every direction, commenting and gesticulating animatedly to her companion, who seemed equally out of place.

"My concierge!" Richard laughed, pointing out the woman to his partner. "After tonight, she'll be in charge of the Grand Tier Left. I thought I'd treat her to the Opéra first, for once in her life, dear creature."

Behind them I rose as if struck on the forehead by a hammer. Of course! He would target Madame Giry's replacement—and I didn't doubt for an instant that he knew who she was. In Nobody's case every wall was an ear.

I quickly surveyed the individuals surrounding the unsuspecting concierge. All seemed as it should be. People on either side of the woman, in front of and behind her, were preoccupied gossiping with their neighbors or perusing programmes. Short of a con-

cealed assassin lying in wait with a rifle, my inventory concluded she was safe enough. I subsided into my chair.

The first violinist now entered the pit to scattered applause and the oboe sounded an A as the other instruments followed suit.

Now the crew working the Calliope dimmed the house lights from three floors below and Leroux himself emerged to a warm reception. He bowed, seized his baton, and gave the familiar *tap, tap, tap* before the downbeat.

Everything proceeded normally. Act I was a huge success with the great de Reszke as Faust, longing to discover the secrets of life and Plançon appearing in a brilliant flash of red light via a trapdoor as Mephistopheles, offering to strike a bargain with him. Arias were enthusiastically encored. Gounod's music, though still too saccharine for my taste, was definitely an improvement on that of Meyerbeer.

My two companions chattered like magpies in an irritating undertone throughout, congratulating themselves on a thousand points, among which they numbered standing up to the Ghost.

"I knew the whole business was folderol," hissed Moncharmin complacently, in a voice that must have carried to the boxes on either side.

"Absolute twaddle," agreed the other in a dull roar.

For my part, however, I knew that trouble, when it came, would arrive in Act II, where Marguerite makes her appearance. But here I was mistaken. The opening chorus, so familiar it seems to have existed since the dawn of time, and Mephistopheles' "Song of the Rat" went down extremely well, with Plançon, let it be said, in excellent voice. La Sorelli made a most favorable impression in the role with which the public most keenly identified her, and before I knew it, the curtain had fallen.

"Excellent! Excellent!" exclaimed those two idiots (Ponelle was right), rising and applauding, but taking bows at the same time,

as though they were responsible for this production, which had, in fact, been entirely conceived prior to their arrival.

Was I mistaken? Had I fallen prey to all the superstition and hocus-pocus around this place? God knows, Watson, here was a situation in which I should have loved to be proved wrong. I breathed easier at the very thought of it. And yet someone had stolen César from under the noses of two grooms, someone kept playing the organ, someone had cut my green yarn, someone had laughed at my discomfiture—and Don José's retractable knife had jammed.

What of it? I asked myself. Mightn't a stagehand have snapped the thread? Mightn't a groom have made off with the horse, or couldn't it have wandered to some hidden nook in this veritable underground city? Could not the laughter as well as the organ have emanated from above and simply travelled downwards via one of the air shafts designed to refresh the animals?

And could not the knife have simply jammed?

But where did the rope that hanged Joseph Buquet go? Were we in store for another macabre exploit or merely one of the Ghost's peculiar pranks?

These contradictory reflections occupied the interval, during which I followed the little concierge and her escort (he later proved to be her husband) into the foyer, where they received complimentary drinks, courtesy of her employer. The good woman was clearly enjoying life beyond her fondest expectations and had not the slightest inkling that I was momentarily prepared to throw her to the ground should any suspicious movement in her direction catch my eye.

But no such movement occurred, and as she drifted back to the auditorium, I returned to box five, arriving there before the general managers. They joined me moments later, carrying glasses of champagne from the bar.

"Enjoying yourself, Sigerson?" Moncharmin inquired solicitously. He proffered a glass filled with tiny bubbles, which I confess I swallowed gratefully.

"The opera isn't over until the soprano has sung," I pointed out.

This observation sent them both into gales of laughter. They convulsed themselves as the house darkened once more, trading barbed witticisms at my expense about violin-playing policemen. I actually found myself pitying the poor prefecture and even Scotland Yard, always being patronized by the folk who would turn to them in pathetic desperation the moment anything went wrong.

Leroux returned to an even more thunderous reception and Act III commenced.

What happened next is so improbable that even now I can scarcely recall it without an incredulous shake of my head. Marguerite, that is to say La Sorelli, is in her garden and she begins to sing the lovely aria "Il était un roi de Thule."

"Ribit!"

Moncharmin and Richard looked at one another. Could we really have heard a frog?

"What was that?" Richard whispered.

Sorelli attempted to continue.

"RIBIT!"

This time there could be no doubt, and, what is more, the frog's croak *emanated from La Sorelli's mouth!*

Still she endeavored to sing.

"RIBIT!"

By this time the managing directors were on their feet and I behind them as well. In consternation the diva clapped her hands over her own mouth, as though to stifle the sound, but when she removed her fingers to resume—

"RIBIT, RIBIT!"

"What the deuce is the meaning of this?" Moncharmin fairly shouted.

The audience, which had responded at first with sounds of mystification, now erupted in pockets of derisory amusement.

"RIBIT, RIBIT, RIBIT!"

"La Sorelli has a frog in her throat!" shouted a wag from one of the balconies, at which the entire place began to laugh and clap hands.

"Give us Daaé!" shouted another, from the Gods.*

"Daaé! DAAÉ!" the crowd began to chant.

"Sing, damn you, *sing!*" Richard called to the poor woman, while Moncharmin mopped frantically at his face with a large cambric handkerchief.

Still the humiliated soprano attempted to comply. She signalled frantically to Leroux, who furiously gestured to those of the orchestra who had risen to resume their places, and they began the aria again.

"RIBIT, RIBIT, RIBIT, RIBIT, RIBIT!"

"DAAÉ! DAAÉ! DAAÉ!"

Finally, the wretched woman could endure no more and, still clutching her throat, fled the stage to tumultuous applause, counterpointed by hoots and jeers.

"Catastrophe!"

"Disaster!" said the directors to each other. "Send for Daaé!"

The curtain dropped abruptly, and the audience now continued in rhythmic unison, calling for the young soprano. We could barely make out muffled shouting and the sounds of pounding feet behind the curtain.

When it rose, finally, it was to reveal La Sorelli's substitute.

---

*The Gods were the cheapest seats, so called because they were so high they were nearest to heaven.

The house was so wild by this time that it was a good half minute before they could be persuaded to take their seats and listen.

Once again the orchestra launched into *Il était un roi de Thule.* Mademoiselle Daaé sang with the simplest and purest expression, as if the music and the words were ideas which had only just occurred to her.

There are different kinds of silence, Watson, especially in the theatre. There is attentive silence, there is bored silence, there is hostile silence, and there is rapt silence.

It was this last expression that greeted Christine Daaé's electric performance. I had to admit that in one respect Nobody was correct. La Sorelli at her best was no match for this girl. Even those two tin-eared mountebanks were stunned into silence by her art.

At the conclusion of the aria the house broke into passionate cheering. They demanded an encore on the spot and received it. This time it was even better.

From this point on, Christine could do no wrong. She went from strength to strength, and the house went with her. I breathed another sigh of relief. Nobody, or whoever he was, had chosen merely to play a bizarre trick. La Sorelli had been ignominiously driven from the stage, to be sure, but no real harm had been done.

In this assumption, I proved to be mistaken.

We had now progressed to the famous "Jewel Song," which Mademoiselle Daaé sang with such artistry that the applause and bravos which succeeded it fairly shook the building. She was obliged once again to repeat the song, and the reception was now deafening.

"Her singing will bring down the house!" came a sudden sepulchral whisper, so close as to let me feel someone's hot breath on my ear. I confess to you, Watson, the hairs rose on my neck at these words. The two buffoons, who had also heard them, now whirled about in panic.

"Who said that?" demanded Richard, trembling and looking at me.

"Not I."

"Not I!" chorused Moncharmin. Their terrified speculations were interrupted by an odd series of tinkles, followed by an uneasy creaking.

All our looks were drawn up towards the sound, as was the uniform gaze of the entire house. We beheld the mammoth chandelier swaying on its moorings. This time the silence in the theatre was of a different variety, a fascinated, hypnotized, almost reverent silence, broken only by the tinkling of ten thousand pieces of crystal and the creaking of the chandelier's harness, which grew more pronounced in the sudden surrounding stillness.

Even though I had a baffling presentiment of what was to come next, a hideous intimation of the disaster, yet I stood rooted to the spot, mesmerized, unable to believe it was to be. Nobody, it seems, was a literal-minded fellow. Frogs meant frogs. And bringing down the house could likewise mean but one thing.

With a sudden tearing sound, the six-ton chandelier broke free of the joists which held it and plunged into the center stalls, landing with such force as to drive an enormous crater into the floor into which it half-buried itself.

The whole could not have taken three seconds, but I declare it seemed a lifetime. The chandelier, as I watched, appeared suspended in midair, the entire house beneath it transfixed by its trajectory, until it plummeted to earth with a thunderous splintering of glass and a mountain of dust.

The shock and noise were so great that the screams which followed could hardly be heard.

By this time, I had recovered my presence of mind and dashed from the box. I raced down the stairs, seven at a time (hoping my ankles would not snap), and tore backstage, where I found Ponelle

standing with the orchestra in joint stupefaction. I seized him by his coat.

"Quick!" I yelled. "Show me the roof!"

"But the people—" cried the violinist, unable to move.

"The *roof,* man! There's plenty to attend to the people." I slapped him lightly on the face. "Take me to the roof!" And I dragged him through the confused orchestra to the door of the pit.

Regaining his senses, Ponelle now understood what I wished, and we plunged through crowds of crying, screaming supernumeraries, soloists, stage managers, and hysterical members of the *corps de ballet* until he located a ladder stage right which led to the flies.

I scrambled up after him, raced down a series of wobbling catwalks and up yet another set of iron ladders leading to wooden gaiters which swayed perilously as we ran along them, and finally up again to the cupola. Down through the hole once occupied by the chandelier chain, we could make out the phantom's masterpiece.

The gigantic fixture had crushed everyone and everything in a twenty-foot radius of the center stalls. People like ants were climbing over each other as they attempted to escape, to assist one another, to free themselves, to die.

I had no doubt that among the victims was a poor woman who had attended the Opéra for the first (and last) time of her life.

And I need hardly add that there was no trace of the monster who had done this thing, only a piece of heavy cable that swung slightly over the aperture, its steel threads frayed where it had snapped, another most convincing accident.

"Is there nothing?" panted Ponelle, staring at me with wild eyes, perspiration streaming down his face.

"Nothing," I answered, pocketing the piece of paper with familiar cursive on it which had been left for me alone.

But I had seen the words: *"Trop tard, Monsieur Sherlock Holmes."*

10

RECITATIVE

"*I* would have done better to hire you for my own protection."

"Never have I blundered so badly."

"I am no more free of blame than you."

"A fine pair we are."

This bitter interchange occurred in Miss Adler's suite at the Grand-Hôtel de Paris, across from the Opéra.

It was the morning following the tragedy, and she was packing for Amsterdam.

The late city editions of *Le Matin, Le Monde,* and *Le Figaro* all carried the gruesome details of the previous night's events. Doubtless the English newspapers reported the catastrophe as well, and you may have read it yourself, Watson: twenty-seven people killed, fifty-two injured, scores being treated for shock, and the Opéra soon to be awash in lawsuits.

The damage to the stalls was being repaired expeditiously and would, so the new management assured the public, be sufficiently complete to function during the Opéra Gala that would conclude the Opéra Masked Ball, said ball to take place as originally scheduled. The management regretted the terrible accident which had occurred but could hardly be held responsible for a misfortune that took place on the first day of their tenure. A new chandelier would soon, etc., etc.

Privately I knew that Madame Giry had already been reengaged for her old position. I doubted the management would ever be prevailed upon to venture near box five again, and I felt certain "Nobody" had had an advance on his monthly twenty thousand francs.

Trunks, portmanteaux, and boxes of varying sizes and descriptions lay strewn open about the suite as Irene Adler's maid trudged to and fro, filling them according to directions from her mistress.

Seldom, Watson, have I felt so culpable, so inept.

"You do yourself an injustice," Irene Adler maintained, when I voiced these sentiments aloud once more. "How could you have predicted such a thing, much less warned those people of their fate?"

"I would have done better to inform the police."

"They would not have believed you, and had you attempted to reveal your true identity you might well have been locked up for a madman."

Her reasoning paralleled my own, to be sure, but at present I was unable to derive particular comfort from the fact.

"I have been beaten."

"You have been beaten before, I think," said she with no trace of coquetry, "and yet have carried the day."

"I cannot bring those innocent folk back to life, whatever I do," I countered gloomily.

"On the other hand," she observed dryly, "you saw to my own salvation. Surely that has some merit, however slight."

I looked and saw a hurt expression on her face, the second time in two days I had beheld in her features something other than her habitual air of amused detachment. I could feel the beginnings of another headache knocking at my temples. Inexplicable, Watson, when you know how rarely they afflict me.*

"Pray forgive me if my remarks have seemed intemperate, Miss Adler," said I humbly. "I thank God you were not harmed."

There was a lugubrious pause as we regrouped our conversational gambits. Miss Adler, seated at her breakfast table, lit a cigarette and poured herself a cup of coffee.

"Why should he wish to kill so many?" she wondered aloud, her thoughts returning to the terrible events of the preceding evening.

"He had no interest in the many, he was interested in only the one."

"You are speaking in riddles."

"Richard's concierge was in the audience. He had given her a pass to the Opéra before she was to assume Madame Giry's post. She alone was Nobody's intended victim. The others meant nothing to him."

Hearing this, her eyes widened in alarm, and she set down the coffee cup with a sharper clink than she intended.

"Do you mean to say that all the other people died merely so that she would perish among them?"

"Precisely."

She allowed herself the briefest shudder.

---

*The repressed Holmes has not made the connection between his headaches and the proximity to the disturbing Irene Adler. Obviously his work with Freud was incomplete.

"I feel I have got off lightly."

"You have." I lit a cigarette of my own by way of keeping her company, and waited. In the bedroom I could hear the locks on one of the trunks snap as the maid fastened them. The noise roused her from the brown study into which she had fallen, and she regarded me once more.

"Do you not find it ironic that the one person in this business who needs absolutely no protection, who is indeed invulnerable, should be the individual I engaged you to safeguard?"

I hesitated. She looked at me, cocking her head to one side in inquiry, as was her wont.

"In my experience of human nature, Miss Adler, devotion so intense as that which Nobody feels for Mademoiselle Daaé is usually separated by a hair from its opposite."

Her countenance darkened as if a stream which had run clear was suddenly clouded by a flood of alluvial deposits.

"You feel him capable of turning on her?"

I said nothing, but she could not fail to read my expression.

"And what do you mean by Nobody? What is Nobody?"

"Has Mademoiselle Daaé never spoken to you of her angel?"

"What of him?"

"Nobody is the name by which the angel is pleased to call himself. It is his voice that you overheard in your dressing room giving music lessons to Mademoiselle Daaé. Originally I entertained the notion that he was a disgruntled employee of the Opéra, but I have been obliged to abandon that surmise."

"What is your present theory?"

"I have none. I know in fact less than he, for he is aware of my identity, whilst I am none the wiser as to his."

She reddened.

"You feel that my outcry may have compromised you?"

Again she perceived me hesitate.

"I am truly sorry for it, Mr. Sigerson. As sorry as I am for having dismissed you as a thinking machine."

There was no doubt of my headache now, Watson.

"Are you certain he knows who you are?"

"Quite certain," said I ruefully, feeling the scrap of paper addressed to me in my pocket. "All I know of him is that he reads Homer." She shot me a questioning look. "In the *Odyssey* the Cyclops, Polyphemus, is blinded by the hero, who calls himself Nobody. When the giant endeavors to name his assailant, his brother Cyclopes are understandably confused." I sighed. "It is his little conceit."

Miss Adler put out her cigarette.

"Very well," said she unhappily. "I hereby relieve you of your charge. And I am heartily sorry to have embroiled you in this affair," she added in a low voice.

Her distress was evident. I pulled up a chair opposite.

"You need not concern yourself on that account, madam. These events would have unfolded in much the same manner had I never interested myself in Mademoiselle Daaé to start with."

This reflection indeed galled more than all the rest, Watson. Before this lunatic I found myself totally powerless.

"I am only sorry to have failed in your commission," I added, after another silence. She stared at me with shining eyes and took my hand, holding it in her own for rather longer than was strictly necessary.

"I pray you say nothing of the kind, Mr. Sigerson. You could never fail in my estimation. Certainly not after yesterday afternoon."

I detected no hint of mockery in her voice or expression. I withdrew my hand from hers gently and rose to my feet.

"About one thing you may rest assured, Miss Adler: I have no intention of abandoning the chase. I intend to bring this villain to book if it is the last act of my life."

"I pray it will not be," said she, also rising, albeit with some reluctance. "May I know your plans?"

"For the present I deem that inadvisable. May I know yours?"

She lifted her shoulders slightly in a gesture I had come to think of as characteristic of her. "After Amsterdam I go to Montenegro." She sighed. "A weary wanderer."

"No doubt you will be glad to quit this place and put this wretched business behind you."

She favored me with an expression very like her old self, looking at me slyly from beneath her silken lashes.

"Not entirely glad, I think. Shall I see you again?"

I took her hand and kissed it; this time I did not let it go.

"All things are possible, Miss Adler."

She searched my face attentively.

"I hope you find what it is you are looking for, my friend."

"He shall not escape me."

"That is not what I meant," she replied enigmatically, and now reversing my earlier gesture, she slowly withdrew her own hand.

THE CITY PLANNING COMMISSION was located at 76 Rue de Varenne, a somewhat narrow thoroughfare with narrow pedestrian kerbs and no trees. Aside from Mrs. Wharton's home, the road was dominated by government agencies.* A clerk seated in the center of the yellow marble foyer of the Planning Commission

*The editor has been unable to decipher this reference.

at the reception desk informed me with an officious, slightly patronizing air that I wanted the Public Buildings Department, which was a hundred paces along the road at number 92.

I repaired to 92, found a more obliging clerk, and told him of my desire to examine the site plans of the Palais Garnier.

"With pleasure, monsieur. All plans of public buildings are open to public scrutiny. There will be a two-franc maintenance fee."

Grateful for this democratic policy, I paid the fee, followed my guide through endless stacks of moldering documents, and waited at the foot while he climbed to the top of a tall rolling ladder.

"Hullo, this is queer."

"Can I help?"

He said nothing for a time, and I waited impatiently while he rummaged overhead, spilling dust and bits of yellowing paper which floated down upon me like so much aged snow.

Finally he descended and faced me with an odd expression.

"They're gone."

"What, all of them?"

He scratched his head by way of answer, then signed for me to follow, and we walked through yet more stacks, only to achieve the same result on another floor.

"Most peculiar."

It did not seem peculiar to me in the least, but I did not say so.

I wondered if I was entitled to a refund of the two francs, but decided, on reflection, not to allude to this, either.

"What about the architect?" I asked, instead.

"Who?"

"Garnier. Have you any idea where I might find him?"

"Père Lachaise—but I doubt he will speak with you, monsieur."

"Why is that?"

He smiled, a bit shamefaced at his joke.

"Père Lachaise is a cemetery, monsieur."

"Ah."

Charles Garnier, it seems, had died two years before and had been buried with no inconsiderable ceremony at the famous grave-site.*

And so another avenue of inquiry was blocked, but an idea had begun to take shape in my mind. I understood now that Nobody's knowledge of the Opéra transcended anyone else's and that he had taken precautions to ensure that no one else should ever learn so much of the place as he already knew. It was unfortunate that the creator of the labyrinth was dead, for, in the absence of plans, his knowledge would have proved most instructive.

I walked the streets of the *rive gauche,* blind with thought as I attempted to marshal my faculties. Doubtless I should have begun my quest for a set of the building's plans before I ever visited Christine Daaé; I should have approached Debienne and Poligny before carrying love notes to the little Vicomte, not after. There were many "shoulds" and not a few "ifs" in my guilty litany. These and other follies besides rendered me culpable, but I realized I should never progress in my investigations if I persisted in dwelling on them. It was easy to be wise after the event, as Irene Adler had intimated. With a resolute shrug of my shoulders, therefore, I resolved to put these matters behind me and start afresh.

My chief difficulty was that in dealing with a madman, the process of logic which usually served me so well was utterly at the mercy of one whose decisions were cloaked in impenetrable mystery. If he was mad, then I must find the method in his madness. If

---

*Everyone famous seems to have been buried there. In addition to Oscar Wilde, the visitor will also find Jim Morrison.

I could not predict his actions, perhaps I could appreciate his motives.

They seemed clear enough, though brief. The monster was obsessed with poor Christine Daaé. This thought, too, began to germinate and grow as I walked past streets and little shops. As far as she was concerned, he was content to make his own rules of life and death, a law unto himself, to come and go when and where he pleased, as if he owned entire the Opéra.

Then it came to me. It was across from Saint-Germain-des-Prés that I experienced my epiphany, as sudden and magical as the apple falling on Newton's head. When I realized my solution I was obliged to stop and lean against a plane tree by the kerb, giddy for a moment with pure astonishment. While incredible, the truth upon which I had stumbled was nevertheless inevitable, and, moreover, had been staring me in the face for quite some time. It was only the peculiarity of it that had prevented my recognition. You know my favorite maxim, Doctor: eliminate the impossible and whatever remains, however improbable, must be the truth. In this fashion only could I account for Nobody's unparalleled mastery of the Opéra's intricacies. I cannot comprehend why the simplest of all explanations had not occurred to me sooner, but in my new mood of self-forgiveness, I chose not to look this particular gift horse in the mouth and waste precious time castigating myself for that which had eluded me so long.

I found Ponelle in his habitual café on the Boulevard Saint-Germain, poring over newspaper accounts of the tragedy with a cigarette dangling precariously from his lips.

"You are well?" I asked, taking a chair beside him and waving for a waiter.

"As well as can be expected," he returned, without looking up. "I wager Madame Giry is back on the payroll."

"I shouldn't wonder. May I ask you some questions?"

He regarded me for the first time.

"Only if I may ask you one, first." I waited. "You knew something was going to happen last night."

"That is not a question."

"Come, come. And you saved Mademoiselle Adler's life during yesterday's rehearsal." Before I could make a rejoinder he pressed his advantage. "I saw you backstage before the evening performance and you were restless as a panther, eyeing everyone and everything." He smiled triumphantly. "And you told me to make your excuses to Leroux. You are a policeman?"

The waiter now appeared and took my order. When he had gone, I made a show of making up my mind.

"I'm going to take you into my confidence," I said finally, and launched into my tall tale about investigating the death of Joseph Buquet at the behest of the prefecture.

Ponelle nodded somberly and flipped some cigarette ash to the ground.

"I knew it." He sighed. "Ask."

"I want you to tell me about Charles Garnier."

"What about him?"

"Can you describe him for me?" He eyed me in some confusion. "His physical appearance. What did he look like?"

Ponelle chewed a knuckle. My coffee arrived, and I stirred in cream with a meditative spoon, endeavoring to conceal my impatience.

"He was, oh, I should say, six feet tall, rather dark-skinned with deep-set blue eyes."

"What else?"

He closed his eyes, straining to form a mental picture, then opened them abruptly with another smile.

"He had the most remarkable head and beard of fiery red hair."

"Would you recognize him if you saw him again?"

"He is dead, monsieur."

"You haven't answered my question."

11

IN THE NECROPOLIS

"**I** cannot believe I have allowed you to persuade me to this," Ponelle exclaimed for the fifth time, as we entered the gates of Père Lachaise cemetery, off the Boulevard Ménilmontant. It was almost five o'clock, and a light rain was falling. Before the young man could change his mind, I took his arm.

"Show me about the place, if you please, and be so good as to remember that I represent the prefecture."

"Then why not summon them on this mysterious errand?"

"It would involve rather a deal of paperwork and publicity, both of which I am anxious to avoid at present. Later, it may become necessary to forgo discretion."

He seemed content with this for the moment, and scowling at the leaden sky, led me up and to the right. The place was enormous, a veritable city of the dead, whose contours followed hills and valleys, crisscrossed by a seemingly endless patchwork of undulating streets and miniature boulevards, all of them populated by tiny buildings, the elegant vaults of the deceased.

"This place gives me the creeps," Ponelle mumbled unhappily.

"You are averse to cemeteries?"

He shrugged.

"It isn't superstition, if that is what you mean. This was the site of the last stand of the Commune, twenty years ago. The most appalling battles took place amongst these very tombs, and many of them were covered by the dead instead of the other way round. The last hundred and fifty survivors were stood up against a wall and shot. They were buried on the spot in a communal grave. It's here somewhere." He shuddered at the thought. "You wish to see where Garnier is interred?"

"I am in no particular hurry. Tell me more about the place," I directed him, seeing that I must distract his attention from my business until I had no choice but to include him in it.

"What would you like to know?"

"Everything. Who was Père Lachaise?"

He shrugged again.

"He was the confessor of Louis XIV and the patron of this place. It was a Jesuit property until their expulsion. The city acquired it around 1800. I'm no expert."

"On the contrary, my dear fellow. As always, you are a font of enlightenment."

We stopped before the crypt of David, the fiery painter and patriot of the Revolution. Nearby I saw was that of Géricault. Perhaps as in Westminster Abbey, the dead were grouped by occupation?

"I don't believe so," elucidated my guide in a neutral tone.

Still making our way in a southeasterly direction, we passed the tomb of Molière, which I pointed out to him.

"It's getting dark; they'll be closing the place shortly," was his only response. "And I'm soaking wet."

"And see, here is Hugo," I exclaimed. "It would seem that writers are grouped together, even as painters." With such banter did I pass the time, only half affecting my surprise at discovering the stone of Beaumarchais and that of poor Maréchal Ney. The place was truly extraordinary.

I lit my pipe and turned the bowl upside down to protect its contents from the precipitation.

"Here is where the Communards were done to death," Ponelle observed sourly, showing me the commemorative wall above the mass grave. In the distance, I heard a bell chiming. The sound appeared to relieve my companion. "Come, we must go. They are shutting the gates. We must return another day to find Garnier."

"Be still. We are going nowhere."

He peered at me through the rain with an expression of incredulity which at any other time I would have found comical.

"Going nowhere. What can you mean?"

"I mean that I intend to see the grave of Garnier this night. Stand behind this of Murger* and do not move until I direct you to do so."

With a gentle shove, I pushed the astonished Ponelle into a place of concealment and took out my watch. How I wished you had been there, Watson! It was just the sort of affair that would have appealed to your intrepid soul, and here I was stranded with a timid fiddle player who was convinced by now that I was perfectly mad.

---

*Henry Murger (1822–1861) was the author of *Scènes de la Vie de Bohème*, which in 1896 became the source of Pucini's opera *La Bohème*.

Unfortunately, even had I had the benefit of your stalwart company, we should still have required Ponelle's unique services.

"But if they find us!" he whispered furiously. I laid a finger on my lips and retained a slight pressure on his shoulder.

As it happened, we had not long to wait. There were few attendants in the place, and in this weather they went about their rounds incuriously, devoting only the most cursory attention to their responsibilities. The dead, after all, were presumed dead. I knocked the ashes from my pipe and put it in the pocket of my ulster, next to the sandwiches I had purchased for the occasion.

It was now quite dark and the breeze had freshened, which did little to improve our spirits.

"I am now ready for you to show me the crypt of Charles Garnier," I announced.

"How could you possibly see it?" he responded with some heat. "I declare, this entire business is most irregular."

"Possess yourself in patience, my dear Ponelle. That building across the way I should imagine belongs to the sexton, who is by now, I wager, home enjoying a warm supper and glad to be out of this inclement evening. Shall we find out if my supposition is correct?"

The little shack indeed proved to belong to the gravediggers, and with no great difficulty I picked the cumbersome lock and dragged my ill-tempered accomplice inside. There, as I anticipated, I found a bull's-eye and several other useful implements, at least one of which I knew would come in handy.

"What do you want with that crowbar?" Ponelle demanded, eyeing it uneasily.

"After you, my dear fellow."

He snorted with something between derision and exasperation and stamped out of the little building.

Following the concentrated beam of the bull's eye, I trudged

in Ponelle's wake as he led me to the northern side of the necropolis. It must have been half a mile. We were muddy up to the eyebrows as we stalked, and once we were obliged to flatten ourselves on the wet pavement as another attendant on his rounds walked past, not three rows to our left.

"Here is Bizet," Ponelle said, fascinated almost despite himself by this time. "The marker was designed by Garnier himself." He was a born tour guide.

"Never mind that now. Show me Garnier."

He gestured. The designer of Bizet's headstone and of the Paris Opéra was interred in a large vault not fifteen paces distant from the composer of *Carmen*. A single word was carved in white granite.

𝕲𝖆𝖗𝖓𝖎𝖊𝖗

I looked cautiously about me.

"Now, my dear Ponelle, I must crave your indulgence a bit further," I said soothingly, as, with a flourish, I produced the crowbar from beneath my coat. His eyes bulged. He had forgot the crowbar.

"What do you propose to do with that?"

"I propose to open the coffin of Monsieur Garnier and to—"

That was as far as I got. Poor Ponelle leapt upwards like a frightened gazelle and made to dive past me. I caught him firmly by the lapels, dropping my instrument with a soft thud on the wet grass.

"Ponelle."

"This is unspeakable!"

"Ponelle!"

"Monstrous! Insupportable!"

"All I wish you to do is identify the corpse."

147

"*What?*"

I repeated my request.

"This is sheerest lunacy! The man has been dead these two years!"

"I think not." He stared at me. "I think Daedalus is still at the center of his maze."

"I have no idea what you are talking about. We shall be arrested and sentenced to—"

"Ponelle, pay attention to me. No one is going to arrest us. By tomorrow evening, we will both be in dry clothing, sitting in our accustomed chairs in the pit and playing at the Opéra Gala. For the present, you must do as I say. These are police orders," I reminded him by way of encouragement.

He sighed miserably but stood by while I retrieved my implement and dumbly held the lantern as I prised open the door of the vault. The task was not difficult; the lock was more ornamental than functional. It yielded to my ministrations with a groan of protest followed by a muffled bang. Signing the violinist to follow me, I entered the vault.

It was chillier within but dry, at least, filled with cobwebs and a disagreeable mustiness.

There were six catafalques from the Garnier clan. The architect's was in the middle on my right, identified by a discreet brass plaque, now oxidized to a dull green.

"Hold the lantern higher."

Mutely he obeyed. The sounds of the crowbar splitting the iron hinges and clasps created a thunderous echo in the little place.

"*Mon Dieu, mon Dieu!* This is barbarous," murmured the honest fellow. Yet despite himself, he had become absorbed by my efforts. Curiosity was his saving grace.

"What do you mean about Daedalus? Who is Daedalus?"

"Once upon a time, before the writing of history, Minos was

the king of Crete," I explained, turning frozen screws now with my stiff fingers. "His wife's brother was a monster, half man, half bull, called the Minotaur."

"Get to the point, why can't you?"

"Just so. His wife loved her terrible brother and could not bear to see him put to death. The king's response was to hire a team of architects to construct a labyrinth and therein to deposit the beast so as to keep him alive while preventing him from harming others. Daedalus was the name of the chief architect."

He thought about this in silence behind me as I worked.

"You think Garnier is the monster? That he created his own maze and took up residence within it?"

"I am certain of it." I pushed at the lid of the catafalque and heard an ominous creaking. Ponelle fearfully drew next to me. "Here, help me push this thing up."

Together we threw back the lid.

"Take the light and tell me what you see."

"I cannot."

"You must."

He squeezed past me with a sudden resolve for which I would scarcely have given him credit and stood on the catafalque beneath so as to get high enough. I heard a terrible exhalation of breath and then he stumbled back, almost dashing the lantern to pieces against the stone wall, coughing a dreadful dry, hacking sound.

"It is he!"

"How can you be certain?"

"It is he, I tell you! See for yourself! Ah, *mon Dieu!*" And he subsided into another fit of coughs, covering his mouth and nostrils with a handkerchief. Leaving him sagging against the wall, I took the light and climbed upon the lower catafalque.

The sight which confronted me I need not dwell upon, though it could not fail to produce a *frisson* even in such a hardy mariner as

myself, Watson. The coffin contained the remains of a tall male in a state of horrific decomposition, the features completely obliterated. Yet Ponelle had been correct in his identification, as the profusion of red hair, which had continued to grow after Garnier's death, made plain. On the basis of its color, the architect might well have been admitted to membership in the League of Red-Headed Men.*

I stood down heavily, shutting my eyes in consternation.

"It is inconceivable."

"What is inconceivable? That a man should lie in his own coffin? Can we now leave this place?"

"One moment." I could not formulate my thoughts, Watson. I had been so certain! My mind, that instrument of my vocation on which I had so long depended and about which I was so pardonably vain, had failed! Numbly I sat on the floor of the vault, heedless of the unforgiving surface beneath me. As is my habit, I spoke aloud, the better to clarify my ideas.

"Eliminate the impossible! The only way in which any man could so navigate the substrata of that building is if he designed the thing himself. That explanation alone accounts for his supreme and unique mastery of the place. He designed it specifically with the idea of accommodating his peculiar needs."

Ponelle looked at me strangely, sinking to his haunches against the wall opposite.

"Is that your theory?"

"Show me a better," I challenged him with some bitterness. He continued to stare at me. "What is it?"

"Only this," he began tentatively. "If you are looking for the architect who designed the Opéra cellars, you've got the wrong man."

*See "The Red-headed League."

"What?"

"It wasn't Garnier. It was his assistant."

"What?"

He nodded eagerly, making himself comfortable opposite me as I gaped at him.

"Of course. He was the real genius behind the foundations. He was the one who figured out about draining the swamp and creating the lake and so forth. Garnier did the theatre proper. It was the assistant who mainly did the rest."

"Icarus."

"What?"

"The son and assistant of Daedalus. Are you absolutely certain of what you are saying?"

"No doubt of it. He figured out all the substructural stuff. A big man with a big laugh. We urchins all adored him. You won't get any information about the building from him, either, though."

"Dead?"

"There was a collapse in . . ." He scratched his head, trying to remember. "In 1874, I think. A cave-in under the Rue Gluck. They had been working on the barrel-vaulted brickwork over the lake. The poor man was buried under several tons of wet concrete and stone. And the building so close to completion," he added, shaking his head at the unhappy memory.

"Buried!" Every time my ingenious theory attempted to stand on its feet, the evidence knocked the pins from under it. "Stop a bit. Did they ever recover his body?"

"Oh, yes, several weeks later they dragged it from the lake bed. I gather it wasn't a pretty sight. Worse than this, I shouldn't be surprised." He gestured with his head to the open catafalque above me.

I knew I was on the right track, Watson, every fiber of my being proclaimed it so, and yet they had found the man's body. Then, with my poor theory once again on the point expiration, another ray of light dawned.

"Did you not tell me once they used to throw corpses in the marsh down there from the time of the Commune, when the unfinished Opéra was used as a prison?"

"Certainly," Ponelle agreed, then opened and closed his mouth. "But you don't imagine, surely—?"

"After enough time in water, the ravages of decomposition may cause one corpse to look much like another. Would you like a sandwich?"

I produced one and handed it to him. Ponelle, wholly engrossed by my train of thought, forgot his terror and distrust and now gave vent to his obsessive curiosity—and his appetite. He took the proffered sandwich as I opened the bull's-eye, and by its restricted illumination we ate for some minutes in a silence punctuated only by the fusillade of raindrops striking the tin roofing above us.

"Tell me about this assistant. What did you say was his name?"

"I didn't, for we children never knew."

I closed my eyes in frustration.

"It wasn't Nobody by chance?"

"Nobody? What sort of name is that?"

"It is English."

"Oh, I see."

I heard him suck air, pursing his lips, trying to be helpful.

"I don't think so. Nobody," he tested the name aloud, but shortly made a negative sound that probably accompanied a shake of his head. "Doesn't ring a bell." Another blow, though I half expected it. "I'm sorry. We simply called him Orpheus."

I opened my eyes.

"Orpheus? Pray, why was that?"

"Oh, he was mad for music. Working on the Opéra was a

dream come true for that man. He would whistle and sing while strolling about the scaffolding as happy and confident as a circus tightrope walker without a net. He had the loveliest voice you can imagine." He snapped his fingers at another memory. "His second passion was mythology. That was the other reason we called him Orpheus. At luncheon he would sit on a rafter or a scaffold and tell us children stories of the Trojan War and suchlike tales from Homer. Orpheus seemed to cover both his manias."

I took a deep breath before I dared speak.

"His voice," I said softly. "A bass-baritone?" He looked at me in wonderment.

"How did you know?"

I said nothing. His eyes grew wider still.

"Do you mean . . . ? But you cannot mean . . ."

"Perhaps it was the shock of being buried alive that caused his reason to give way. But one thing is certain: he survived the collapse. And he has chosen to live in the Opéra ever since, refusing to show himself."

I could almost hear if not see the wheels of Ponelle's brain ponderously beginning to grind as he endeavored to make sense of what I was saying. I heard him crumple the paper wrapping of his sandwich.

"But why? Why not show himself?"

"I confess I have not the remotest idea. I have insufficient data at present to answer that question. I can only attribute it as a feature of his mental collapse. Those who claim to have laid eyes on him are unanimous in speaking of his ugliness. Was Orpheus ugly? Deformed in any way?"

"On the contrary. He was a fine figure of a man. The ladies were terribly fond of him."

I shook my head, unable to account for the phenomenon.

"Perhaps it is only people's fancy that he is horrible," Ponelle

went on, musing to himself as much as me. He was evidently remembering Bela's theory about Beauty and the Beast and how
women in particular always preferred the hideous monster to his
handsome reincarnation.

I said nothing as the rain continued its intermittent tattoo
above us. Suddenly I snapped my fingers.

"No, he is a monster, sure enough, and it was the cave-in that
made him one. How slow I have become, how rusty, Ponelle!"

"What do you mean?"

"Nothing, we policemen are always highly self-critical. Only
take my word for it, Orpheus was disfigured as the result of the
collapse. That is why he never leaves the opera or shows himself."

It took but a moment for the idea to register with him.

"But, do you really think such a thing can be?"

"At present," I threw out my hands, "it is merest conjecture.
I postulate all of this as unproven theorems. Let us suppose, for the
moment, that Orpheus has carved out a private fiefdom for himself
in the bowels of the place and reached an accommodation with the
management, who finance him. He lives undisturbed and at peace
for years in his lair. All was well enough until three months ago,
when he heard and then saw a young soprano."

"La Daaé?"

"He fell in love, and woe betide those who wittingly or otherwise stand between him and the object of his passion."

I refilled my pipe, affecting to ignore Ponelle's amazed gaze.
His ruminations now turned up something else, and this troubled
him, for he frowned.

"But what of Carlotta and the frog in her throat?"

I struck a match and puffed vigorously before answering.

"Have you never heard of the art of ventriloquism?"

He shook his head.

"It is an ancient but obscure trick, dating back at least to

Roman times, though currently practiced only by Gypsies and fairground performers, a sort of oral *trompe l'oeil*. The word itself means to speak from the stomach. It is not generally known, but a skilled practitioner may 'throw his voice,' that is, cause it to appear as if it emanates from someplace other than himself. Adepts can even manage it so that their lips do not move, but in this instance our man had no such need. What is more, with the apparatus in the Opéra at his disposal, it would not have been difficult for him to amplify his frog creak—using the echoes of the air shafts from the roof, for example, or other tricks we cannot guess at. He has had years to perfect his technique," I added, remembering the disembodied laughter. Ponelle passed a hand over his mouth as he endeavored to understand what I was telling him.

"You are saying there was nothing wrong with Sorelli's voice?"

"Nothing whatever. The villain had only to interrupt her with his cruel substitution every time she opened her mouth to sing."

"This, all of this, is—" He groped for the words and huddled deeper into his shabby coat, suddenly chilled by something other than the dankness of the vault.

"Preposterous? Consider, Ponelle, it is the only theory which explains all the facts, the only explanation for his uncanny ability to move throughout the Opéra at will, seeing and hearing every word that is spoken. He alone is familiar with every nook and cranny. Why? Because he designed them all himself. Fortunately," I added, "though he knows the Opéra like the palm of his hand, his kingdom is limited by its boundaries."

We sat in silence for some moments longer. Then Ponelle spoke, shifting his position uncomfortably, his voice oddly constricted.

"I wouldn't be too sure of that," he began with a certain tentativeness. "If what you say is true."

"What do you mean?"

"You have heard of Baron Haussmann, the builder of Paris's great boulevards?"

"Of course."

"But you may not know of his other achievement—the one in which Haussmann took even greater pride."

"To which achievement do you refer?"

Ponelle pointed downward with his finger.

"To the largest and most modern sewer in the world."

"What?"

"It extends the length and breadth of Paris, monsieur. And if Orpheus has access to it—"

"He can wander at will beneath the city!"

"Precisely."

In my apprehension I stood as if pulled by invisible wires.

"Where are you going?" he called after me as I ran from the vault. "What shall I do with Monsieur Garnier?"

12

NEAR TO HEAVEN

*P*onelle, out of breath, caught up with me at the side gate near the Avenue Gambetta. The big lock there proved no more difficult to spring than that of the sexton's shack. I firmly resisted all his questions.

"Say nothing of this to anyone," I told him as we walked briskly down the deserted road. "Forget what you have seen tonight."

"That's easier said than done," the wretched violinist fumed, his testy humor rekindled now that we had put some distance between ourselves and that macabre place. "We've opened up a great man's coffin and left him lying about."

"He is still in hallowed ground," I countered cheerfully. "I am certain no harm has befallen his immortal soul, and his earthly remains have assisted the cause of justice. Come, here is a cab and you are wet to the bone. Go home, have a good night's sleep, and I will see you tomorrow at the Opéra Ball."

He was cold and tired enough to do as I instructed.

"What will you do now?" he asked from inside the cab.

"I am soaked, as well," I pointed out. "Drive on, cabby!"

It took me rather longer to find another cab at that time and place, and I own I was frigid by the time I regained my lodgings, but the cumbersome expedient served my turn; a second cab enabled me to avoid Ponelle's inquiries, which were commencing to come as thick and fast as raindrops.

Once in my digs in the Rue Saint-Antoine, I peeled off my sopping garments and threw on my old dressing gown. As the resources I needed next were not at my disposal until dawn, there was nothing for it but to try and sleep. This I fear I was unable to do. My mind insisted on racing back and forth over the data I had accumulated and the use to which I intended to put them. This was no mere busman's holiday, Watson. My quarry had killed almost thirty men and women in the twinkling of an eye, with no more thought than if that chandelier had been a flyswatter. I confess to you, my dear fellow, that this was the only time in the whole affair when I longed for the soothing consolations of the needle. I lay in bed imagining the morphine silently stealing through my veins and bringing me a torporous peace.* In ruminating about the narcotic and its effects, I must have found a kind of ease, for soon it was daybreak.

Once again, time was my enemy. I had bungled my previous attempt at cutting out the heart of this mystery and resolved at all costs not to fail in a second try. Nevertheless, the hours I had at my disposal to form and execute my plans were few. I could have used your help, Doctor, and ruefully contemplated the circumstances which deprived me of it.

*It is generally thought that cocaine was Holmes's drug of choice, but before his drug cure with Sigmund Freud, it is also true that he had sampled and enjoyed morphine, as well. See *The Sign of Four.*

It was after three the following afternoon when I arrived at the Rue Gaspard. As I knocked on Mother Valerius's door, I was chagrined to observe an elementary fact which had altogether eluded me on my previous visit. In my eagerness to interview Mademoiselle Daaé, I had failed to note that the rooms she shared with the elderly invalid were on the ground floor. This made perfect sense for Mother Valerius, who could not otherwise enter or leave her lodgings without assistance, but it also put the two women within easy earshot of a determined listener. Armed as I was with Ponelle's chilling intelligence regarding the pervasive Paris sewer system, I could readily conjure the presence of the Ghost, the angel, Nobody, the canary trainer, Orpheus (his list of aliases stretching now as long as my arm), crouched beneath Christine's very bedroom, assisted perhaps by something as simple as a doctor's stethoscope planted against the wall, privy to every word the poor girl spoke. No wonder he appeared to know her most intimate thoughts! I need hardly point out to an experienced medical man such as yourself, Watson, that when one sense is deprived, the others work overtime to make up for the one that is gone. Buried in something like perpetual darkness, it was not hard to imagine that the monster's hearing had become acute.

At first she refused to see me. The little maid brought word both ladies were indisposed. I fear I was short with her and (once again) gained entry by the threat of force. I stopped at the bedroom of Mother Valerius, who implored me to go no further.

"Two days! I have never seen her like this, monsieur. She is ill, too ill to receive you!" Her lace cap trembled on her head as she spoke.

"I am afraid I have no choice but to insist, madame. I understand Christine is unwell, but if she is to regain her health she must trust me implicitly."

Her features registered surprise.

"You are a physician?"

"In this case I merely know how to cure her, madame." I kissed her hand and withdrew before she could press me on the subject of my credentials, and found Christine sprawled across her own small bed, wearing the dark blue dressing gown I had admired before. She lay on her back, her hair unbrushed and unpinned, tumbling about her shoulders, one arm flung across her face, her entire form convulsed by terrible sobs.

"Christine."

"Go away!"

"Not without you."

Recognizing my voice, she removed her arm briefly and surveyed me with a tear-stained countenance before concealing it once more, this time burying it in the folds of a pillow.

"Go away," she repeated in muffled tones.

"Mademoiselle Irene Adler would never forgive me if I did." But even the invocation of her trusted friend failed to penetrate her despair.

"I am lost."

"So you are—unless you follow my instructions to the letter."

"It is no use!"

"Do as I say."

Something in my voice brought her up short. She propped herself up on one elbow in a defiant attitude, tossing her tangled locks about her.

"He has done nothing wrong! It was an accident!"

"Then why do you weep? Besides," I went on, before she could answer, "you know perfectly well it was not. Did you not tell me of Nobody's promise that your singing would bring down the house?"

Her features crumpled, and she threatened to collapse again. I seized her by the arms and shook her roughly.

"Get dressed. I need you."

"Where are we going?" she asked as I handed her into the brougham I had kept waiting before the door.

"As far from the ground as I can manage."

Her eyes widened at this, but she said nothing during the ride. She barely glanced at the city outside the window, hardly took in the passing spectacle of Paris going about its daily life, but when she did look, it was with a startled regard that suggested one who saw very little of what you and I would call everyday activity, Watson. So much his creature was she that her experience of life was as circumscribed as he could devise. Her little room, her studies, her prayers, her journeys to and from the Opéra, her carefully selected performances—these and these occupations alone constituted the small world into which he had squeezed her delicate spirit. Her existence was almost a parody of a prodigy's sheltered regimen. It was at the least a bizarre mirror image of *his*. They were both of them trapped in worlds behind walls—his were external, hers only existed in the confines of her enfeebled mind.

When the brougham stopped and I handed her to the ground, she looked up fearfully, her color quite gone.

"What is this place?"

White clouds in an azure sky scudded quickly past the distant spire.

"Surely you know. You have seen it often. It is visible to all Paris. Come with me," said I, gently but firmly taking her arm and paying off the driver.

She was as skittish as an unbroken colt, every different sight and sound a shock to her delicate nerves. Crammed into the enormous lift with dozens of strangers, she quivered next to me like a vibrating tuning fork and gave a little cry when we lurched to a start and clutched my arm in an iron vise as the cogwheels bore us upward in a gradual arc.

At the first level we switched into a smaller lift. She followed, mute with terror as the ironwork flashed by the window like lace, increasingly spare and delicate as we climbed ever higher.

There was a third lift, half the size of its predecessor, and for a moment I toyed with the idea of staying where we were, but there were too many people for my taste. I wished to see everyone around us for miles. I could not be certain but that the monster had a confederate following us even now. It was certainly clear that someone delivered the things he bought with his monthly stipend—else where did his food come from and how had he acquired and assembled the component parts of his organ?

She was shuddering like a leaf when we emerged at the summit but allowed me to lead her up the steps to the small outer terrace, where the wind snapped the brim of her bonnet.

"Why have you brought me here?" She tried closing her eyes at the sight of all Paris spread out beneath her in every direction, but the attempt must have disrupted her equilibrium, for she opened them again almost at once.

"Because here we are free of his power. The closer we get to heaven the less he can control you."

"He is an angel!"

"Devils, we are told, make their homes underground, not angels."

"But his opera, *Don Juan Triumphant,* his masterpiece—it is almost finished!"

"It is finished already. Christine, you were meant for this"—I gestured with my arm, throwing it across the horizon—"a world of sunshine and laughter and people, a world with Raoul in it," I concluded somewhat prosaically. "No angel would ever dream of asking you to surrender that happiness to which every human heart has a claim."

"What is it you want?"

"I want you to sing tonight, at the gala following the Opéra Ball."

"Never!"

"You must!"

"I could never get out a note, I tell you. Not without my angel to prompt me!"

"Look at this beautiful city! Look at the blue sky and shining sun and tell me you need anything but your own genius, Christine.

"You labor under a misapprehension," I went on in a milder tone. "Your voice is your own, and you can sing whether he wishes you to or no."

"But you saw what happened to Carlotta! You heard!"

"Let me disabuse you of the notion that Carlotta had a frog in her throat." I attempted to explain again the mysteries of ventriloquism, but she clapped her hands over her ears.

"I cannot understand," she protested frantically. "You use too big words!"

"Then understand this," I shouted in return, seizing both her hands in mine. "Your only chance for freedom and for happiness is to break the unnatural chain which binds you to this Lucifer!"

She said nothing for a time, then walked some little distance past me, towards the railing. I tensed, ready to fling myself upon her should she take it into her head to clamber over the barrier.*

For a time she stood thus, her back to me.

"You wish me to betray him," she said at length in the toneless voice of one in whom the bright promise of hope has been utterly extinguished.

*It wasn't until several suicides had taken place that the Eiffel Tower was modified to discourage jumpers. (In later years also, the number of elevators required to reach the summit was reduced from three to two.)

"I need you to draw him out, yes."

"How do you know he will even be there?"

"He knows you have been taken from his reach. He will have to see for himself where you are and what has become of you. And besides . . ."

"Yes?"

"He cannot resist a touch of the dramatic. It is a cast of mind with which I am familiar."

There was another interminable pause. Still she did not turn. When she finally spoke it was in the listless voice of one already dead.

"Tell me precisely what it is you wish."

13

UN BALLO IN MASCHERA

Nowadays the Opéra Masked Ball is what is known as a "charity function," Watson, and there are those who would insist that this bourgeois alteration has robbed the entire affair of its essence. Twenty years ago, in its heyday on the fateful evening when I attended it, the Opéra Ball was in its final flowering, almost the last event of its kind on a social calendar that was even then vanishing forever. A stolid Victorian sensibility would soon steal across the Channel (despite the occasional patronage of the merry Prince of Wales), and would contrive to dry up the rivers of permissiveness that flowed on such nights in favor of middle-class propriety. Older participants would maintain that the pleasures of respectability were no pleasures at all.

Because the Opéra Ball of yore was held by and for the Opéra, it was of the theatre and therefore one of the few soirées where the *haut* and *demi-mondes* met and publicly overlapped. Singers, after all, were a species of actors, and Henry Irving had not yet been knighted, conferring an unimpeachable respectability on that ancient profession. It was no quirk of character that had caused the elder de Chagny to frown upon his brother's attachment to a soprano; it was an inbred social instinct. Perhaps if Philippe had suspected a mere vulgar intrigue he would have been more tolerant. It was love that made the thing a blemish.

At the Opéra Ball, however, all such distinctions were waived for the duration. Not only were the participants culled from two slices of society that were often pale with envy of one another, they were also masked, and this anonymity provided for and indeed encouraged every sort of intermingling.

There is something about being anonymous, Watson, as I had occasion to observe at the time, which loosens the constraints upon one's character in a fashion that could be called vertiginous. At the outset of this history, I endeavored to describe my sensations at the prospect of my own incognito and the dizzying possibilities afforded thereby. It may seem that my use of such prospects was relatively tame compared with the opportunities exploited by those at a masked ball. I, after all, had merely decided to become a violinist, and, as we have seen, even in that unremarkable calling, I was unable to avoid being overtaken by my true *métier*. Others effected more radical departures from their identities, albeit for shorter periods of time. (The longer one remains anonymous, the more one's true self emerges despite all efforts at concealment.)

Indeed, the action of obscuring one's persona behind a domino at places like the Opéra Ball granted every sort of license. Those who by daylight were inhibited by custom or age suddenly found (with the aid of a glass or two of champagne) that they were capable of the most outrageous behavior. Provided only that their masks never slipped, they could reflect with wonder in the days to come on their unbridled conduct. Then again, there were those already

familiar with the phenomenon, who looked forward with eager anticipation to the rites of the night. These were the roués who premeditated and relished what the traffic would bear on such occasions, and who prepared for it.

Lest you suspect me of embroidering, my dear fellow, I need only point to the plots of countless operas to illustrate my thesis. *Die Fledermaus* of Strauss the Younger is the quintessential example of such indulgence at a masked ball, wherein a respectable married man unwittingly attempts to seduce his own wife because both are incognito—she disguised as a singer, a sure invitation to indulge in scandalous behavior. Mozart's *Figaro* and his *Don Giovanni* make use of a similar device, albeit for more exalted purposes. In Verdi, masks and their consequences are almost a continuous theme.

The Opéra Ball was divided into three parts. (Like Gaul, I hear you say, Watson!) The first was held in the main foyer and on the enormous grand staircase. This consisted of drinking and mingling and dancing and was followed by the second event, the Opéra Gala, wherein the partygoers became an audience and assembled in the theatre for musical excerpts performed by the most celebrated artistes of the day. Afterwards, all repaired again to the foyer, which had, during the performance, been converted with tables for an enormous sit-down midnight supper.

Invitations to this event were amongst the most eagerly sought in Paris, in France even, for couples and individuals who were lucky or powerful enough to receive the coveted white cardboard with the almost indecipherable calligraphy—(and who would never dream of attending any opera!)—descended from the provinces, sartorially equipped for the occasion. They stayed at the best hotels and there changed into their costumes, trading pheasant shooting for other game.

As a member of the orchestra, my invitation was automatically conferred. I limited my own disguise to evening dress and a black

domino. I was not alone in this choice. Many men had no desire to encumber themselves with elaborate and unfamiliar clothing. A simple mask would serve their turn; why should they trouble themselves with extras? My inclinations by way of costume were not limited to preference. To the members of the ensemble that was later to perform, Maître Leroux had given strict instructions as to dress.

We were, however, in the minority. The majority of the guests were attired in every sort of disguise. I saw Harlequins and Colombines, Marie Antoinettes (with full-rigged sailing vessels in their coiffure), at least six Napoleons, three Jeanne D'Arcs, (one of whom was tied to a stake which she carried on her back), several Pierrots, a Cardinal Richelieu, an Henri de Navaare, two Sun Kings, Aztec warriors, Greek virgins, Roman senators, and members of the animal kingdom—a lion, a vulture (with enormous wingspan), even a griffin, to say nothing of donkeys, horses, and cows (which required two sets of legs to man them). In addition, there were giants on stilts (lucky because they could see over the heads of the rest), and dwarves and trolls, walking on their knees and cursing themselves for not having foreseen the consequence of their ingenuity, burial alive amongst a forest of legs.

Bolder participants appeared as Eve and Adam or Lady Godiva, long, thick tresses and large fig leafs providing modesty and decorum where needed (and suggesting, in the case of Adam and Eve, that these impersonations took place following the Fall). I marvelled at the *sang-froid* of the Garde Républicaine, who struggled to remain immobile in the face of these licentious temptations as they were pushed and shoved about by the seething mass.

Some participants I recognized despite (or perhaps because of) their dress. Moncharmin and Richard were attired as the Mad Hatter and the March Hare, respectively, *and* with, I suspected, no intimation of irony. The *corps de ballet,* including the mischievous little Jammes and her rival, Meg Giry, were unsurprisingly in their

tutus, choosing to take advantage of the opportunity of displaying their shapely limbs to a host of admirers at close range.

The entire throng mobbed itself to the point of immobility and produced a jostling riot of color that would have piqued the interest of Degas, had he seen it. Now that I mention the fact, I am sure that among the guests was more than one artist, who, if he could remember his inspiration in a day or two, would doubtless attempt to render the scene. The noise created by the shouts and laughter easily drowned the music provided by a small band at the top of the grand staircase. Only the sound of a drum and trumpet intermittently succeeded in piercing the din.

The heat was terrific, and though the foyer was enormous—it gave one the idea that some befuddled brain had crossed Paddington Station with a Greek funeral vault and sprinkled the results with mosaics from Ravenna—the sheer volume of human bodies drenched with the varying scents of assorted perfumes gave one the olfactory impression of being in a Turkish bath run amok. Even those who had had the foresight to attend more or less nude were bathed in perspiration. And yet one could not escape the conviction that the whole place had been conceived for just such events as this.

The crowning touch of visual chaos was provided by two nymphs, hired for the occasion, who, dressed in togas, stood above the shapeless mob on opposing balconies and methodically showered all and sundry beneath with handfuls of confetti which they gathered from large shallow bowls tucked into their waists. They performed this function without any manifestation of emotion save a Teutonic thoroughness, which resulted in a veritable blizzard of red, blue, yellow, pink, white, and green bits of paper raining down upon the frenzied guests, falling into open mouths, adhering to elaborate coiffures, and sticking to damp bare shoulders.

As I had promised her I would, I kept my eye on a certain

Dresden shepherdess caparisoned in yellow skirts and sky-blue bodice, both trimmed with red piping. She advanced tremulously amongst the press, making her way with the aid of a large shepherd's crook. She paid little heed to the multitude, moving as if in a trance, save for an occasional jerk of her head in one direction or the next. She ignored the flirtatious remarks and gambits which trailed in her wake, except to snap her head away after listening to some apparently too bold suggestion. Poor Christine! Where was she going? Alas, she had not the faintest notion, though she was clearly persuaded her judge and jury were hot on her trail.

Gradually I became aware that she was being followed by someone other than myself. A tall Pierrot in whiteface and clown mask, one dark tear painstakingly drawn on his left cheek, was even now rapidly closing the distance between himself and the shepherdess. Could this be my prey? I moved forward as fast as I dared, but I had not reckoned with the density of the mob, which impeded me as if it were a wall of brick.

From over the tops of heads twenty feet away, I saw him approach, take her arm, and whisper in her ear.

She twitched at the sound and turned into his embrace, which caught her fast. Despite her attempts to extricate herself, his arms pinioned hers. I could see her writhing desperately to free herself from the unwelcome imprisonment, her mouth below her mask grimacing with the effort.

"Christine!" I called, but my voice, if they heard it above the babble, made no difference to either of them. He pulled her further from me, and shortly they vanished, absorbed into the recesses of the throng.

Cursing myself for having allowed such a distance between us, I lunged forward, brutally throwing people aside in my zeal to overtake them.

In the midst of my vain efforts, a piercing scream broke through the babble and silenced the entire foyer.

It was little Jammes, visored but still recognizable atop the shoulders of a circus strongman, pointing with a trembling arm.

"The Ghost!" she yelped, and screeched like a banshee once more.

"The Ghost!" echoed a voice I knew to be Meg Giry's. It emanated from an East Indian princess, carried in the arms of a Puritan greybeard.

All followed the direction of James's shaking finger, and the crowd gave a collective gasp.

At the top of the grand staircase was an enormous figure sheathed in scarlet from top to toe, his death's-head visage crowned by a large hat with scarlet egret plumes. His form was swathed in a voluminous cape of the same hue. Even from where I stood, I could perceive the malevolent glitter and flash of his eyes behind the mask.

"The red death!" cried a voice, and some folk obligingly added their screams to Jammes's.

A cry of woe that I recognized as Christine's decided me. It sent a shiver of conviction which shot me through in an instant as I beheld my quarry at last. It wasn't Pierrot. He was of this earth, merely the monster's confederate, whose existence I had already surmised. The giant at the top of the stairs, standing as still as if he were made of iron—this was the canary trainer.

In another instant, I had made my choice. Given the chance to pursue Christine or the creature who had blighted her life, I unhesitatingly chose the latter. This mass murderer—for he was nothing less, Watson—was my true game, call me heartless or what you will.

Making no further pretense at politeness now, I dove into the mob and tossed aside obstacles to my goal as if people were so many matchsticks.

The phantom in scarlet remained motionless but an instant longer, then whirled about with a huge arc of his cape and swept up the stairs.

The frozen moment had passed. Someone's laughter broke the spell of immobility. The band resumed playing and the crowd recommended its frenzied steps leading nowhere.

Then, out of the corner of my eye, I saw Pierrot release Christine and likewise make to follow his master, energetically tugging at those who stood between them in his eagerness to effect his escape.

For their part, the mass of humanity in the midst of whom these events were unfolding remained happily oblivious to them. So many folk were being pulled and pushed that one or two ruder examples made no particular impression. In my case there were those who pushed back, giving as good as they got and laughing into the bargain.

It was no laughing matter to me, as you may imagine, Watson, but an affair of the utmost moment. Realizing that I would never make my way through the ocean of confetti-strewn revelers, I turned the other way and ran for the opposite staircase. Here the crowd was more diffuse. I raced up to the Family Circle in time to see the giant in red fleeing down a passage a hundred feet before me. I ran as I have never run before, barreling through the band, whose instruments exploded into the air as I passed, careering across the corner just in time to see that capacious swirling cloak disappearing on the other side of the theatre, heading downstairs.

There were faint cries and sounds behind me now, but I paid them no heed, so possessed was I with my own purposes. I had a pretty fair idea of where the rogue was making his way, and rather than plow through all the champagne drinkers on the Family Cir-

cle, I again retraced my steps and, regaining the foyer, used the door I knew would take me down to the dressing rooms.

My intuition was rewarded by the sight of both of them—the scarlet giant, trailed by the Pierrot—speeding down the deserted corridor before me. The footfalls of my boots sent reverberations shouting down the narrow passage after them like reports from a revolver. I put on every ounce of speed I had, and my lungs were fit to burst when I saw first one and then the other dodge into Christine Daaé's dressing room.

Gasping for air as though I were drowning, I tore through the door just behind Pierrot, in time to witness a stunning flash of silver mirrors that momentarily blinded me with their swirling reflections, and then, impossibly, I found myself alone, heaving for air, my lips beneath my domino flecked with foam.

As I stood there, bent double struggling to regain my breath, the pounding and cries in my wake drew nearer. The door to the dressing room was thrown open so violently that it ricocheted off the wall behind it. In less time than it takes to tell, the place filled with a half-dozen men, two of whom seized me roughly and drew me to my feet while a third tore off my mask.

"Monsieur Sigerson!" exclaimed Moncharmin, removing his own disguise. "What is the meaning of this?"

"You know this gentleman?" demanded a slender figure in a red, silk-lined opera cape. He removed his own mask, revealing hard, humorless features and a slight pencil mustache.

"Yes, indeed, Monsieur Mifroid," Ponelle exclaimed, looking at me guiltily, his honest features creased in consternation. "He is the man who claims to be looking into the affair of Joseph Buquet at your instigation—but he was engaged by the Opéra three weeks before the murder occurred. I knew something was wrong," he added, almost as if he were trying to explain his actions to me rather than to the slender policeman.

"I see." Mifroid strode near to where I stood, helpless and gasping like a spent racehorse, and looked me up and down as though he were examining carrion, a barely detectable sneer playing about his lips.

"Allow me to explain," I began, but got no further. The crowd smelled my blood.

"He demanded a set of plans for the whole building!" shouted one.

"He tried to catch Christine at the ball!" cried another.

"He assaulted Mademoiselle Adler!" offered a third.

"Gentlemen, listen to me, please."

"Be silent! Monsieur Sigerson, I am placing you under arrest."

14

ORPHEUS'S UNDERWORLD

"*Y*ou must let me speak!" I insisted, struggling vainly with my captors. "While we stand here a tragedy may be unfolding!"

"A tragedy *has* unfolded," Mifroid reminded me, coolly continuing his inventory of my person.

My position was untenable, Watson. One by one they testified against me, remembering the questions I had asked, the stories I had told to excuse them, my disappearance from the orchestra the night the chandelier had fallen, and a thousand other inconsequential details which of themselves meant nothing, but which taken as a whole seemed to form an ominous chain and made things appear black against me. Moncharmin and Richard, absurd in their ridiculous attire, solemnly proclaimed my guilt, recalling my visit to their offices, which they now remembered as a series of threats on my part. With a certain low cunning, the two scoundrels had perceived the advantage of laying the blame for all that had happened at someone's door—anyone's door—before the lawsuits began to fly.

Never had I found myself in such a predicament. It would have been risible had not my circumstances been so pressing. I had no idea where Christine Daaé was, but she was to sing shortly, and I had promised her my protection. Now fate had placed in my path the one unforeseen obstacle for which I had been unable to make provision.

I was unceremoniously bundled forward through the multiplying crowd which now jammed the dressing-room corridor, making it virtually impassable. I had no doubt that once I was removed from the premises there would be nothing and no one to stand between Christine Daaé and the wrath of her lunatic guardian.

Here, Watson, was the terrible price exacted for my incognito. Just when it would have most benefitted me to claim my own name and identity it was simultaneously the furthest it had ever been from my reach.

"Where are you taking me?"

"The gendarmerie."

Again I protested my innocence and the urgency of the situation. This time no one even troubled to reply.

Somehow we forced our way to the end of the corridor and were about to start up the stairs when Fate, which is capricious in all things, took yet another turn.

"Where do you imagine you are going with that man?" cried a *basso profundo*.

Blocking the path to the steps, his hands on his hips, his great bull's head fixed in a stubborn attitude atop his massive torso, stood Maître Gaston Leroux. I confess I was never so pleased to see anyone in my life.

"We are taking this man—"

"Be silent. This man is going nowhere." He glowered upon the multitude with a look of concentrated ferocity.

"But—"

"I am Gaston Leroux!" he roared. "I am responsible for everything that happens here. The smallest detail does not escape my attention. I am in complete command." This familiar refrain caused me to sigh with relief, but Mifroid was not so easily deterred.

"I beg your pardon, *cher maître,*" said he in a patronizing tone he little seeked to disguise, "but this gentleman belongs to the law."

Leroux clapped his pince-nez atop his nose and stared frostily through it at the policeman.

"You are in error, monsieur; permit me to disabuse you. This gentleman belongs to my first violin section, and we have yet the Opéra Gala before us. Let me make myself quite clear," he continued in stentorian tones before anyone could interrupt him. "I am not interested in the Ghost. I am not interested in murder or the law or any of the trifles with which you people concern yourselves. Your affairs are your own. If you wish to set a guard over this man while he discharges his obligations to me, you are free to do so, *but*"—and he gave the word a terrible emphasis—"my business, my only concern, my religion, and my responsibility is *the making of music*—and anyone who attempts to interfere with that obligation will find himself doing so over my corpse."

He paused, daring them to dispute with him. Mifroid himself appeared a little stunned by Leroux's peroration.

"Does one violin make such a difference?" he made so bold as to inquire in a peevish voice.

"The last time it went missing the chandelier fell from the roof," Leroux shot back in a very civil manner.

"It wasn't Sigerson," Ponelle piped up, eager to ingratiate himself with me after his denunciation. "He didn't even know how to get up there."

"But he did go up there," Mifroid reminded everyone, fingering the brim of his silk hat and evidently thinking the matter over. "Very well, *cher maître*. Deferring to your needs, I will allow this gentleman to perform this once—but under guard, you understand? Under guard."

Leroux inclined his massive head in acknowledgment of the terms.

"And afterwards, he is to come with me," Mifroid announced to all within earshot.

"Thank you," I managed to say as I was escorted past the conductor.

"Thank *you*—for saving Irene Adler, the loveliest mezzo-soprano of our age, from extinction!" he called after me.

I was now bundled in the opposite direction and soon found myself in the familiar surroundings of the past few weeks, that place which had played silent witness to the happy period of my life during which I had endeavored to reinvent myself. Now it would shortly witness my ignominious success in that undertaking. I had entered the pit a detective on holiday, amusing himself with a career as a violinist; I would be leaving it as an impostor under arrest for suspicion of murder.

I suppose, Watson, that things were not truly so bleak. I would have an attorney; I would summon witnesses to my character and identity from across the Channel—you, for instance, my dear fellow—witnesses who would be astonished to learn that I was still alive. The whole absurd tapestry would be unravelled sooner or later, thread by thread.

But in the meantime, long before then, the wretched woman to whom I had promised my best efforts, whom I had persuaded

against every instinct in her body to trust me and to sing this night, would be without my promised protection.

The gala entertainment portion of the Opéra Ball was about to begin. The merrymakers, having slaked their thirst with many a glass of champagne and having tired themselves by standing virtually immobile for upwards of three hours, were now grateful for the chance to sit down, even if it meant listening to an hour's excerpts of so-called serious music. They were a bit drunk, but that did not affect Maître Leroux's mania for perfection. Drunk or sober, he would give them the best the Paris Opéra had to offer. That was, as he had said, his *raison d'être*.

The crater caused by the impact of the fallen chandelier in the center stalls had been more or less repaired by workmen toiling round the clock. It was a temporary solution which would wait on a permanent one following tonight's performance, but chairs were in place over covered scaffolding and the whole area had been touched up with carpeting and gold paint.

The programme for the gala was traditionally a surprise. Those of us involved backstage knew it well beforehand, naturally, but there was no printed notification for the audience. Instead, Maître Leroux reserved for himself the privilege of announcing— or not announcing—the treats in store.

There was hardly any need for the house lights to dim on this occasion, as the main source of illumination in the auditorium no longer existed. Instead, torchlight flambeaux had been installed, each with a liveried attendant, which lent the proceedings an eerie, somewhat barbaric atmosphere, as if the revelers found themselves in an enormous Roman amphitheater or bear pit.

Understanding the inebriated temper of the place, Leroux made no announcement for the first number, merely gave the downbeat, and the curtain rose on the "Soldiers' Chorus" from *Faust*.

This was exactly the sort of thing the revellers wanted to hear. They cheered and stamped, and some sang along with the familiar tune, humming or whistling, as most did not know the words.

Immediately following, with no interruption, the orchestra played the "Rakoczcy March" from a different *Faust,* this one by Berlioz. This extraordinary piece had the effect of working the house up to a fever pitch of exhilaration, and the cheers and bravos which followed it told the conductor that the merrymakers were now with him heart and soul. They thought they knew him inside out. He was a jolly fellow, this Leroux.

But the *maître* had anticipated and confounded their expectations when the curtain rose again.

This time it revealed an empty stage, with only depictions of the stars in the heavens. The great Plançon, as Mephistopheles, defied the heavens in the prologue to yet another *Faust,* this one by Boito. "Ave Signor!" he commenced mockingly.

From the moment I heard these first words, however, I knew— as did Leroux and a good many others—that this was not Plançon. By no stretch of the imagination could these towering howls be ascribed to the familiar bass-baritone. The astonishing power, Watson, the sheer terror of this defiant Lucifer with his credo of damnation, was sung with a vehemence and sardonic vitriol such as I never anticipate hearing again, this side of hell.

"Who the devil is that?" exclaimed Ponelle.

Leroux mopped his brow, a concession to his own astonishment, but he continued to conduct. He may have had no interest in ghosts, but he knew the sound of genius when he heard it.

From the gasps of the audience I knew that we were not alone in our reaction. On my left I thought Bela's eyes would pop out of his head. I did not need to see who was singing to understand that it was none other than the canary trainer himself—the Ghost, Nobody, Orpheus, the Angel of Music—all his titles now woven trium-

phantly into one! How I should have loved to launch my pursuit then and there, but it was out of the question. I played under the watchful eyes of two gentlemen from the prefecture who did not once attempt to view the activity onstage. They knew their duty and obeyed like the trusty mastiffs they were. Perhaps they were deaf.

At the conclusion of the aria, the house was stunned into total silence. Mephisto, never removing his death's head, took his bow and, gathering his cape, which he threw nonchalantly across one enormous shoulder, sauntered insolently from the stage, departing with a flamboyant grandeur that defied applause.

What had become of Plançon?

And where the deuce was Christine? Had she heard Nobody's performance? Or had she fled when the apparition first appeared atop the grand staircase?

Or had she never even got the chance? Had the monster abducted her before he went onstage? Apprehension contained me in its icy fingers like a vise. There is a certain kind of fear, Watson, that seizes its victim much like a gathering frost, rapidly immobilizing the limbs from top to toe so that the mere act of putting one foot before the other all at once becomes a veritable labor of Hercules. Despite my best resolve, it was this sort of fear that spun itself about me cocoonlike as I fiddled like an automaton.

"I'm sorry," whispered Ponelle, during a burst of applause.

"It is not your fault, my dear fellow. You did what you thought best," I responded as by rote.

"I couldn't explain your story, you see," he protested. "I knew you had started here before the murder of Buquet—and then there was all that nonsense at Père Lachaise."

"I quite understand." And truly, how could I have done otherwise? Were I to put myself in Ponelle's place, what would I think had someone asked me to swallow so transparent a fabrication? It had been good enough for Debienne and Poligny, whom Ponelle rightly characterized as idiots, but Ponelle himself was not a fool, and I had blundered badly in mistaking him for one.

I noticed the torches were burning out. So much for improvisation. It was a lucky chance they hadn't set fire to the building. In any event, Miss Adler had been correct when she had quoted the dictum that the show must go on. Even now, in the confusing aftermath of Plançon's disappearance and his inexplicable, if sensational, replacement, the programme continued to unfold with no deviation or hesitation, like a train on its tracks, obeying an immutable timetable.

The curtain next rose on the greatest success of our current season, the skaters on genuine ice from Act III of *Le Prophète*. For this performance workmen in the flies dropped snowflakes upon the *corps de ballet*. The effect was a triumph of illusion, and the audience sat enrapt, many having never seen the thing before, nor having anything to compare with it, for that matter.

Now Leroux faced the audience.

"Mesdames et messieurs." His familiar bellow had no difficulty in penetrating every corner of the place, from the stalls to the Gods. "Mademoiselle Christine Daaé."

The curtain rose on a blank stage. Mademoiselle Daaé, still dressed as a shepherdess, though now unmasked, stood alone, a shawl draped artlessly over her shoulders and a basket over one arm. So she was still at liberty! I might somehow yet save her!

"Sigerson, sit down!" Leroux hissed, and tapped his baton as always before the downbeat.

She sang tentatively at first and I could hear the terror in her voice, but as she went on it seemed the music itself sustained her as I had told her it must. She had chosen Micaela's prayer from Act III of *Carmen*. The only genuine aria in the piece, it was ideally suited to both her voice and her looks. As it happened, it was equally suited to her present frame of mind, for it depicts the supplication

of a terrified woman, alone and at the mercy of forces beyond her control, who begs God for His divine protection. The extraordinary music bore her voice aloft, clear and clean as the pure mountain air which supposedly surrounded her. I could see from Leroux's rapt expression that she had totally transported him—and if she was having this effect on the conductor, I did not need to guess what the audience made of her performance.

Again the music was followed by silence. But this time a lone "Bravo!" led the response by a fraction of a second. From my vantage point I could see the entire house rise as if catapulted together from their seats. Christine Daaé had triumphed again, this time without any assistance but her own equipment, skill, and taste.

She came forward to the apron, where we in the pit could see, and acknowledged the contribution of Leroux and the orchestra with a graceful gesture of one arm. She stood in a kind of a daze and curtseyed low before the adulation, hunching her shoulders slightly as she was pelted by flowers from every direction and shouts of "Encore!" reverberated throughout the hall.

And then, with no preamble or warning of any kind, the lights went out. They did not dim or flicker but died all at once, as though a single switch had been thrown at the Calliope. The entire theatre was plunged into total darkness.

The applause, which had seemed as if it would endure forever, quickly dwindled and was replaced by cries of alarm. Recent events of a terrible nature in this very place were instantly recollected by one and all, fuelling the panic of the blinded assembly.

The moment the lights vanished, I had risen again. In the confusion I was certain I had heard a single scream.

As suddenly as they had been extinguished, the lights were restored. Though it seemed an age, the entire eclipse could not have lasted more than four seconds. Yet it was sufficient.

Christine Daaé had disappeared. All that remained was the

basket she had been carrying on her arm. The poor prop sat by itself, alone in the vast expanse of empty stage, its singular presence a mute harbinger of a new disaster.

The impudence! The audacity of it, Watson! What a *coup de théâtre*! He had sung magnificently before three thousand people, defying them to apprehend him or arrest him or merely to identify him, and then, adding insult to injury, right under their noses (to say nothing of the noses of a contingent of police), he had snatched her away! I could not help but admire him for it, even as I cursed my confounded impotence in the face of this faceless genius, this No-body.

But I knew I would never get another chance. The game was afoot,* and if I did not give chase at this very instant, my prey would go to ground forever, and he would take Christine Daaé with him.

And I had no illusions that, like Persephone, she would ever be returned to the world of the living.

My limbs thawed abruptly from the constriction into which fear had confined them, and I exploded through the door to the pit, the flabbergasted policemen splitting apart before me. I could hear their astonished yells behind, but I never slackened my pace.

Once more I tore down the corridor towards Christine's dressing room, which I now understood to be the frontier for which I had been searching since the beginning of this business. Once inside the little room, I locked the door behind me, pocketing the key. Outside, I could hear the thudding feet and excited voices of my pursuers.

I blocked out everything but the task at hand, focusing my mind on one object only—finding the hidden door or panel through which Nobody and Pierrot had passed moments before I

*The game's afoot! This catchphrase, long associated with Holmes, is actually Holmes quoting from Henry V, "Once more unto the breach!" etc.

had caught up with them. I had seen only a swirl of spinning mirrors, but that brief glimpse was sufficient to inform my search. The dressing-room door was subjected to a barrage of pounding as I ran my hands up and down the reflecting walls, pressing here and there, sweat running into my eyes and stinging them as I grunted with the effort. Somewhere on or near one of these surfaces lay concealed the trigger that would unbar my way to Nobody's domain and all the secrets of this tangled business. If the dressing-room door gave way to my pursuers before I discovered it, all was over for Christine Daaé.

At the last instant, my labors were rewarded. One corner of a mirrored panel surrendered to my tentative touch and a low rumble proclaimed the presence of an invisible counterweight on the other side of the wall. With no time to think how I should return, I dashed through the hidden aperture, even as the panel revolved on its axis and slammed shut behind me. I bent over, hands on my knees, catching my breath, conscious at the same time of the dressing-room door being broken apart, not ten feet from where I stood. The audible splintering of wood was followed by startled exclamations on the part of those who were certain I should be found within. There was a confused babble of voices, attempting to reconcile the locked door with my disappearance. As I foresaw, one light, brighter than the rest, took it that I had locked the door from the outside and fled, leaving them to smash it by way of gaining time. This theory was quickly adopted and the hounds died away, leaving me free to look about me and examine my surroundings.

I had indeed found that for which I had been searching when I was arrested. Not the false, but the true entrance to Alice's rabbit hole; a kingdom within a kingdom, a sort of contiguous universe which existed alongside all else in the Opéra substructure and yet remained separate and inviolate, except upon the whim of its creator. Christine Daaé's dressing room was the crossover point be-

tween the two. Possibly there were others, but I had need of only one: Nobody's remarkable creation, his exclusive network of paths and doors, of chutes, ladders, tunnels, bridges, scaffolding, and steps, lay open to me at last.

I had no thread to unwind, nothing to guide me but a single instinct which told me I must always head down. Descend! Be like a drop of water! When in doubt, descend! I had one clue only, and that was the burning stumps of candles stuck at various strategic points, some still lit, others yet warm, which the fugitive had used to find his way. Feeling where the candles were placed, I invariably found huge deposits of coagulated wax. The man had had years to perfect his giant hidey-hole, and many lights had guttered themselves here before these.

I appropriated one of the candle stumps for my own use and by its meager flame I groped my way, the hot wax burning my fingers and congealing on them, for I had nothing with which to shield them.

I heard sounds, mysterious echoes, drops of water and strange, distant footfalls, either above or beneath me, I could no longer tell. Much of where I walked was scaffolding and catwalks which bisected vast empty patches of gloom. Sometimes there was a handrail of sorts with which to steady myself; other times there was nothing; to make matters worse, my footing wobbled beneath me.

In the distance I saw a pair of moving lights and thought I heard voices. I crept forward cautiously, conscious now of every creaking timber underfoot. From behind a set of wooden slats I glimpsed the Calliope, the tremendous gasworks machinery that controlled all the lighting in the Palais Garnier. It was another crossover point between what I had come to think of as the real world and this, its depraved simulacrum.

The police were at work, mere inches from me, puzzled by the

three corpses they had just found—the poor souls who worked the levers and dials of the lighting panel, dispatched to heaven by the maniac.

"Their throats are slit," said a voice I recognized as Mifroid's.

"This one's skull is crushed," said another.

"It is Mauclair!" exclaimed a third, which I knew to be Jérôme's. Between them they were trampling every clue in sight. I shook my head and withdrew as carefully as I had come.

Down and down. Sometimes I strayed from the path and wandered up what proved to be curious *culs de sac,* though for aught I know they led to still other secret passages by means I had not the time nor skill to discover. In these instances I was obliged to retrace my steps, stumbling over objects and choices which were second nature to the deranged proprietor. My poor stump of wax burned to nothing and I was again enshrouded in blackness.

Once I held my breath as a troop of rats, intent on their own errand, scurried past me on a narrow platform. I could feel their slight forms skittering across the tops of my boots, and it was difficult to suppress a shudder.

Down and down and down! I tried to keep track of the levels as I thought I knew and understood them, but in truth the path declined but slightly and in the darkness I soon became disoriented. I no longer was able to determine what was above and what below. The very walls no longer struck me as purely perpendicular. Gravity alone was my compass.

As I navigated this singular route, I could not but ponder the evil genius behind it. What single-minded determination and ingenuity had created first one world and then managed to fit a second inside it? Or had both worlds been conceived simultaneously? What dark purpose, what inspiration or desperation, had driven Nobody to such a magical, almost miraculous feat of engineering?

And how much time had it taken—or did time, as I had begun to suspect, mean nothing to him, voluntarily immured here for the term of his own existence?

As I felt and tapped my way, I became gradually aware of a sound which, superseding the miscellaneous noises which caught at my consciousness like so many grasping fingers as I passed, finally dominated all the rest. It was a distant, intermittent thudding, which grew louder, then ceased altogether, then recommenced. I had no idea what this could be but soon had more or less incorporated it as part of my map. When I was heading deeper, it mounted in volume; when I erred, it faded and grew faint. Something about the sound, or more particularly about its irregular rhythm, was familiar, but I could not place it at the time.

Going at my tortoise's pace, it seemed hours before I came before an enormous iron door, though the darkness very likely gave me a prolonged sense of time. The distant heavy thudding, having grown stronger, now abruptly ceased, leaving me in a cavernous stillness. I ran my hands over the door and rapped it with my knuckles, producing a dull echo. I concluded the thing must weigh hundreds of pounds and despaired of my ability to move it without uncovering the secret of its mechanism. I searched for what must have been the better part of two hours without result. I threw all my feeble might against it then, and, as I anticipated, the iron did not budge. Impossible though it might be to admit, it seemed my journey had been in vain. Once again the creature looked to have eluded me.

Faced with this insupportable prospect, I sat on a brick plinth and leaned back with a great sigh on the object of my frustration, trying to digest my disappointment and consider any alternatives which might occur to me.

The strains of a long and eventful day must have told, because the next thing I remember is waking up in the same place I had sat

down, and the cause of my waking was also my salvation. In my sleep, I must have twisted my back sideways against the panel, for, to my astonishment, the entire assembly yielded to the mildest pressure and slid noiselessly on rails off to my left, causing me almost to fall through the opening. I recovered my balance and spent some moments struggling to recollect where I was. I seized my watch and tried to make out the time. It had just gone five, but this meant nothing to me. Five in the morning or at night? Was it possible I had really slept so long? Here was no way to tell.

Then I realized I had light to read the dial, and this caused me to look through the aperture my tossing and turning had created.

The sight which greeted me on the other side of the sliding door was one I should not soon forget. I see it still, sometimes, in my dreams.

I had succeeded in gaining the underground lake. It stretched away beneath a series of barrel-vaulted brick ceilings and huge supporting columns which disappeared beneath the surface of the mist-covered water obscuring the farther shore. An echoing hiss proclaimed the whole chamber to be lit by gas, siphoned off, I daresay, from the Calliope above, where the murdered men lay.

I knelt and touched the water and was surprised to find it tepid. No doubt its warm temperature, emanating from deep underground and coming into contact with the colder air of the vault, was responsible for the perpetual mist which clung to its surface. At the same instant my fingers disturbed the liquid (which had an unpleasant, greasy texture), I was startled by a nickering sound and looked up to behold a large white horse, seemingly revealed through an uneven rent in the fog.

"*César!*" I cried. The beast seemed in no way discomfited to see me. Moving closer, I determined he was tethered by his bridle to an iron ring attached to a post, which in turn was planted on the small margin. A basin of fresh oats occupied a brick shelf before him.

Next to the post was a slip, large enough, I judged, for a small dory or pinnace, though I could find no trace of either. It was no great matter to infer that the boat had been taken by its owner to the farther shore—wherever that was.

I decided to employ the horse where the dory would have been preferable and untied him from his stake. He followed me placidly enough, and though he had no saddle, did not demur when I led him alongside his provender and used the brick ledge which supported it to give me a leg over.

"Now, César," said I softly, guiding him towards the mist. "Can you swim? Can you take me across the lake?"

The water was, I have noted, warm, and the horse did not object to its peculiar feel. He planted his feet carefully along the brickwork where the slip was constructed and eased himself gracefully into the steamy liquid.

I had no terribly clear idea of where we were going. I could only hope César was better informed. He began swimming with powerful undulating strokes. The mist divided before and closed directly behind us. The experience shortly began to assume a certain dreamy enchantment. I had to pinch myself to remember I was less than two hundred feet below one of the busiest intersections of a bustling metropolis and that a woman's life hung in the balance of my quest.

I had begun to suppose we were making good progress when the gas which provided the place with its faint and eerie glow dimmed and went out, leaving the animal and myself stranded in the middle of the subterranean body of water with no idea in which direction to go or indeed if we were going in any consistent direction at all.

The horse whinnied in fear. I leant forward and patted his neck to comfort him, but I was far from easy in my own mind. The ominous thudding now resumed, more strongly than before. At

first I thought I should be able to use the sound to guide us, but quickly determined that, thanks to the peculiar acoustics of the place, the noise appeared to emanate from everywhere at once. The irregular pounding echoed heavily betwixt the water and the brick, doubling back on itself, bumping into itself and producing a chaotic cacophony suggesting—in my present mood—that I was on the inside of a madman's wildly beating heart.

We swam aimlessly for some minutes, bombarded by the echoes, but then the sound stopped yet again, leaving us in darkness and silence more terrible than before. Now the only sounds César and I could discern were our own.

15

THE MILK BOTTLE

*H*ow long we paddled thus I cannot say. The horse collided once with one of the circular brick columns supporting the vaulting and, in his terror at finding his head briefly underwater, very nearly threw me.

We were rescued by the sound of an organ. It began softly enough for us to sense its direction. As we headed towards the sound, the music enlarged and soon was joined by a familiar bass-baritone—and then I heard the clear soprano of Christine Daaé. She was alive, though frightened, as I was able to deduce by the tremolo and vibrato in her singing.

The duet was unfamiliar to me, but even in my own confused state I recognized its surpassing beauty, though there was too much reverberation amongst the stones for me to make out the words. At one point the song stopped altogether and I feared César would

lose his compass again, but after a brief interval it resumed, starting up at the same measure as before.

With a stumble and a scrape, the horse found his footing and we pulled ourselves out of the warm, greasy water. At more or less the same time, the oddly familiar thumping recommenced, much louder now even than on the lake. With each crash on this side of the water, the ground itself trembled beneath us, as if giants were at play near the place where we stood shivering.

My trousers were sopping, but everything above my waist was relatively dry. I found my matches and struck a light, holding the tiny flame above my head.

On the ground before me I perceived several dark patches. I squatted and touched the nearest of these. It was wet and sticky. The flame burnt my fingers and I dropped the vesta; lighting another, I knelt close to the stain, which under illumination confirmed my worst fears: it was blood.

Leaving César where he stood, his reins scraping the earth, I crawled forward, the music obliterated by the crashing and shaking, as I followed the crimson trail with the aid of a succession of matches.

The splotches increased in size and led me to the body of the Pierrot, who lay on his back in his white silken clown garb with three comically large dark woolen buttons on the front of his loose smock.

Though wounded, the man was still breathing. I lit yet another match (I had but three remaining) and examined his face. The paint which had covered it was now smeared with perspiration and the backward swipes of his right sleeve, revealing his features.

"Monsieur le Vicomte!"

He opened his eyes. It was indeed Christine's suitor, de Chagny the Younger.

"Raoul, do you remember? It is I, Sigerson." I tore off a bit of his costume and made a tourniquet around his wound. The match had gone out now and I was obliged to work in the dark.

"Sigerson," he said faintly, then I felt him stiffen, remembering. "Where is Christine—?"

"She's alive, my dear fellow. Listen, can you hear her voice? She is alive and down here somewhere. Can you sit?"

He grunted in pain as I righted him and held my shoulder so forcefully I thought I must cry out. His hands were like ice.

"What is that terrible noise and shaking? Is it an earthquake?"

"An earthquake that starts and stops. How did you reach this place?"

"I returned from the country the moment I read about the chandelier," he began. "My brother tried to prevent me, but I was ashamed of my craven performance the night you visited us and determined to make up for it. I knew Christine must feel dreadful about all those unhappy people who perished listening to her sing. I went first to her rooms and thence to the Opéra Ball, where I found her. I tried to get her to leave with me. She was desperate to escape and kept trying to warn me off, but I held her fast."

"Until you saw the fiend," I offered.

"How did you know?" In the darkness I could feel his suspicious eyes upon me.

"I too was on her trail. I mistook you for one in league with him."

"Then you saw him too!" he cried hoarsely, seizing my lapels. He went on as if remembering events which had taken place years and not hours before. "He was standing atop the grand staircase, all in red, and I heard one cry out that it was the Ghost. Forgetting my original intention, I left Christine and pursued that villain who was the cause of all my griefs. He sought to escape me through her dressing room, but I was too quick and followed him—" He broke

off, coughing violently and pinching my shoulder again. "Until I got lost in this infernal maze. How is it the very walls, the ceilings, the floors all obey him as if he made them?"

"Because he *did* make them. Can you stand? We have not far to go to beard the creature in his den. Try. Try!"

With an effort I dragged him to his feet, and we squinted about us in the gloom, the ground trembling beneath us like the treacherous deck of a ship about to founder in a tempest.

His arm around my neck, de Chagny yelled close to my ear, "I've heard this noise before!"

His sentiments echoed my own. The noise and quaking were maddening, but even more so was the notion that I ought to know what they were. César whinnied in terror with each convulsion.

Then, as was its wont, the crashing ceased, bathing us in silence except for the music, which drifted towards us in the near distance.

On his feet, after resting on my frame for several moments, the little Vicomte was actually fitter than on the ground. As more air penetrated his lungs, he grew stronger, and we staggered forward towards the ravishing harmony, which now lay directly in our way.

On this side of the lake, a double wall contained the mass of water, the layer between filled with earth to give it support. Following the curve of the dam towards the music, we came upon Nobody's house, for it literally was a house, constructed between the inner and outer walls that embraced the lake. There were lit windows with proper curtains drawn across them; the structure looked like a miniature palazzo on the Grand Canal. On the other side of the windows the singers were still engaged in their rapturous duet. In silhouette we could make out the seated organist and Mademoiselle Daaé's form, standing beside him. The Vicomte was struck dumb by the sight and might have been capable of something rash, but I urged him forward.

Moving further along the wall we came to what must be another chamber of the place, this one without any fenestration whatever.

"Perhaps there is an opening from above," I hazarded. "Can I give you a leg up?"

"Give me your matches, first."

I made a step for his shoe by interlacing my fingers. With an effort he clambered over my back to the top of the wall and examined it. The crashes and shakings recommenced at their haphazard intervals around us. There was too much noise to hear a match being struck, but I detected a brief flare of sulphur before he reappeared above me.

"Come up. There's a skylight of sorts with illumination beneath it."

This was no easy feat, for I had no one to help me and the Vicomte was too weak to pull me from above.

"Wait here," he instructed, and shortly returned, gasping for breath. "Use this."

He unfurled a rope, one end of which he had tied off someplace above me. The other dropped near my head, and I seized it. A few moments in the dark, running my fingers along it, were enough to satisfy me. I could feel quite plainly where it had been sliced by a razor-sharp blade.

By use of the murder weapon of Joseph Buquet, I was able to hoist myself alongside the Vicomte, who led me to the skylight-like window, which was really more akin to a ship's porthole. A peculiarly thick glass oval was surrounded by a brass frame on a hinge.

"Can we fit through that thing?" the youth asked dubiously.

"It is open," I pointed out. "We have little choice but to try."

The aperture was indeed a slender one, but I was able to slide through it and catch the Vicomte when he came after me.

"Fool that I am," I muttered when we had landed.

"How do you mean?"

I pointed to the ceiling and the little window, now out of reach above us. In my eagerness to penetrate Orpheus's stronghold, I had forfeited the practical aid of the rope, which I had unthinkingly left behind.

The room in which we found ourselves was again illumined by hidden gas jets, even as the lake. It was hexagonal, mirrored from floor to ceiling and decorated by the multiplying images of a large wrought-iron tree, whose reflected branches caused a forest of illusion to appear around us. The design was disorienting in the extreme, doubtless the effect its designer had intended. There was no entrance or egress save the small opening through which we had come. If we had supposed we were gaining access to the monster's dwelling by employing this route, we appeared to have been mistaken. Just below the ceiling and all around the hexagon, I detected a series of small holes, each about the size of half-florin.

"They must supply the air," suggested the Vicomte.

I did not like to contradict him by pointing out that the window through which we had entered already satisfied that need. The holes to my mind were sinister and made me uneasy. For that matter, the entire chamber seemed to serve no purpose except to trap unwary folk who tumbled into it, much as we had, rather like an empty milk bottle set outdoors to snare flies.

"Listen," I said. "The music has stopped."

We put our ears to the mirrored panel through which the sounds had been heard most clearly. I discerned what sounded like a door closing. Then nothing.

"Call her," I whispered.

"Christine."

"Louder. She cannot hear for the din outside."

"Christine! Christine, it is I, Raoul! Can you hear me?"

There was a faint sound from inside the wall.

"Who is that?"

"Christine!"

"Raoul? Oh, Raoul!" Furiously pressing our ears to the mirrored glass, we could make out her sobs.

"Christine, where is he? Where is he?"

"Raoul—go away! Leave this accursed place at once! Ah! He's returning! He's—"

Now another voice.

"What are you doing there? Come back. We must perform the last-act finale. What? Does my appearance still terrify you? There is naught to fear, I tell you. Come to me. I say come!"

The voice was at once supplicating and threatening, as if its owner could not make up his mind what attitude to strike.

There was another crash overhead that caused everything to tremble. I heard an angry snarl on the other side of the wall, and then the voice, softer:

"Don't be frightened. They cannot harm you. None can harm you anymore. You were wrong to sing tonight without my permission, my love, but I forgive you. Only remember: I know what is best for you and for your voice. Sing with me now."

His lulling cadences almost caused my eyes to close. The music resumed. It was hard to make out with the other sound, but in the pockets of silence we listened. It was of transparent beauty.

"What is it?" Raoul whispered.

"His opera, Don Juan Triumphant."

The poor boy gave a sob of horror and exhaustion and sank to the floor of the place, weak from loss of blood. I remained with my ear fixed to the glass. By and by the music concluded.

"This shall be your home," said the beautiful voice softly. "You must be tired. I will leave you. Rest now."

I did not see how she could rest, for the wretched shuddering was now taking place in earnest. As it was impossible to communi-

cate with the poor girl over its din, we were left to our own devices,
which were few. The hexagon was bare of any object save ourselves
and the iron tree, or rather merely the trunk and one single
branch, for the rest was all reflection.

As time passed, the young Vicomte began to lose his nerve. His
teeth chattered uncontrollably, and placing his hands over his ears
in a futile attempt to stop the noise and shaking, he cowered on the
floor in a corner of the place and commenced rocking to and fro,
making little whimpering sounds, like some frightened animal. I
tried to comfort him with soothing words, but understood him to
be rapidly passing beyond the bounds of reason.

"Vicomte! Raoul! Call Christine again. Here, the noise has
stopped! Call her! Ask her to describe the room. How many doors
are there?"

He was unable to hear me.

"Lieutenant de Chagny, I have given you a direct order!"

This locution succeeded where gentler attempts had failed.
The training of the École Naval asserted itself, and the youth leapt
to obey the commands of a superior officer.

"Christine!"

"Raoul! Oh, my love!"

"Christine!" cried the desperate boy. "Is there no doorway
between us? Can you not find—?" Their conversation was interrupted by a clang and a shout.

"Raoul!"

"So!" cried a terrible voice. The girl screamed.

The sound of another door slamming, and we waited, the little
Vicomte trembling as one with ague.

"So," repeated a familiar baritone above our heads, gentle as
a sigh. "Here are unbidden guests."

I looked up toward the sound, and beheld the little overhead
window filled with an ivory death's head.

16

NOBODY

The fragile remainder of the Vicomte's resolve escaped him at the sight, and he fainted dead at my feet.

The creature and I stared at one another for what seemed an interminable period. I felt myself to be almost mesmerized, now that I had come this close to those glacial features.

"Will you not remove your mask?" I asked, at length. For a time he said nothing. I began to imagine he had not heard me.

"I cannot," he returned finally, his voice a mellifluous hush that might have originated in a cave.

"I entreat you."

"It may not be." He seemed to hesitate. I almost believed I could detect the glitter of his dark eyes staring at me from behind the protection of the mask. "Were I to do so, I should be unable to speak."

"Why is that?"

"It has ever been thus. Since I was a child. My mother forbade me to speak without my mask. 'Do not speak without your face,' she instructed me always. Now I have become so accustomed to the conjunction of the two that I am dependent upon it."

My expression of surprise at his answer evidently reminded him of his errand.

"I hope you will forgive this intrusion," said he in dulcet tones that fairly ravished the ear with their tenderness, "though I regret I am unable to forgive your own."

"Monsieur Edouard LaFosse, is it?"

The eyes blazed up in a moment behind their place of concealment, like coals before the bellows in a distant fire, and then as quickly subsided. I fancied, however, that I was still the object of a venomous regard.

"I am Nobody."

"Would you prefer to speak in English?" I offered, taking my cue from his name in my attempt to buy time. Again he hesitated.

"I would prefer not to speak at all."

"But you were Edouard LaFosse," I persisted. "The brilliant assistant of Monsieur Garnier."

He regarded me through his expressionless face. "The men you speak of are dead," he observed with heavy finality. "Nobody alone survives. As you, unfortunately, shall not."

"You were clever to destroy the plans of the building," I continued, still hoping to distract him. "But you did not think to eliminate the contracts, which include your name on them. I found them at the City Planning Commission before I called upon Mademoiselle Daaé yesterday afternoon."

He grunted at this and revolved his head as though relieving an ache in his neck. Or was he casting a look over his shoulder?

"Was that your opera I heard just now? *Don Juan Triumphant?* I am a musician, you know. I thought it exceedingly fine. May I hear more of it?"

"You are Sherlock Holmes, whom the world already supposes to be dead," he answered with something hideously like a smile in his tone. "Your cumbersome guile is wasted on me. Under these circumstances you will hardly be missed," he added. His magical voice was like steel caressing satin.

"You must know she can never love you. She pines for this poor young man." I gestured to the unconscious Vicomte.

The creature craned forward briefly to observe his rival.

"She is young," said he calmly. "She confuses infatuation with affection, but her art teaches her better. *I* have taught her better. When he is gone she will forget and love again only her Angel of Music."

There was an intense crash now, and the whole building tottered. He snarled with a fury so abrupt and terrible that I started, raising my arms in front of me, even as my legs sought purchase on the slippery glass flooring. But his rage was directed at the sounds rather than myself, whom he indeed appeared to have forgotten entirely, as he clutched the frame of the little window opening for support.

"Her angel is a devil who has committed the sin of murder," I reminded him when the shaking had ceased. "She cannot undo that knowledge," I went on, "and it will doom you."

He made no reply to this but looked down upon me with what I imagined was a most pitiable expression of melancholy stamped upon his motionless features.

It was amazing to me that his rigid countenance was capable of assuming varying aspects. No doubt the effect was entirely the product of my own fevered brain at the time.

"We shall see," was his eventual and succinct reply. He vanished and the window was fastened from outside.

There was silence now, save for the rumblings all about us. I knelt and tried to revive the Vicomte. I was in the act of bringing him round when I noticed that the mirrored floor of our cell (so must I call it) was wet. Looking at the glass before me, I saw that a thin sheet of water was cascading down the front of it, collecting at my feet. In fact, all the walls were now crying silent streams of water from the spouts near the ceiling.

"Vicomte! Raoul!" I slapped him lightly two or three times, and he opened his eyes.

"What has happened?"

"If we do not act, we are to be drowned." I gestured to our plight, and he scrambled to his feet in alarm.

The water was rising faster than one would have supposed from its silence. We sloshed about the chamber, leaning on the walls, kicking at them—all without result.

"Christine! Ah, Christine!" sobbed the youth, flinging himself again and again upon the partition which separated them.

The only conceivable device that might assist us was the iron tree itself, and this I set about prising free, even as the villain indulged his favorite trick of turning off the gas. In the dark the Vicomte began to scream with terror. I had all I could do to get him to help me snap free the ironwork as the water gathered about our knees.

From the chamber next to us, the Vicomte's cries were submerged in the boom of the organ, upon which Nobody was favoring us with a Bach toccata and fugue.

Finally, after we had furiously bent the thing to and fro, the iron prop tore lose in our blistered hands. With the water around our waists, it was harder to move, but we commenced smashing the

iron against the glass, which shattered about us, the shards settling on the liquid and drifting languidly to the bottom.

Running my hands along the places where the glass had been, I could feel wood panelling. Even as the entire place shuddered with the continuing earthquakes, we took turns jabbing our instrument against the wall of Christine's chamber. It was difficult to detect any headway, save a few splinters, for the water had now risen above our chests, making it almost impossible to manipulate the heavy object.

"We are doomed!" cried the Vicomte. I was in no position to dispute him. The water was now below our noses, so that we would soon be obliged to swim.

"Don't let go the iron!" I cried, for I could now see our only hope was to make use of it to smash the window above us, when the water carried us high enough to reach it. This was easier said than done, for the thing was quite heavy and threatened to drag us under with its weight.

I was now directly below the porthole-like entrance to our prison, with scarcely an inch of air left between me and the glass. With every ounce of strength remaining, I endeavored to bring the iron branch against the window, but without success. The designer had foreseen the weakness in his plan and had made sure the glass was thick and secure. It was impossible, in our position, to bring anything like the force required to shatter it. The outcome could no longer be in doubt.

As the Vicomte and I were totally submerged, another quake shook our prison, and this one succeeded where all our frantic attempts had failed. Very likely the fiend had not calculated how much pressure the walls surrounding us would have to bear should the hexagon ever be completely filled with water. Added to this, the shaking of the place must have dislodged a buttress, for, with a sudden rush, the level lowered abruptly and we were sent spilling at

a tremendous rate into a room I had barely time to see before it, too, was engulfed in a liquid avalanche.

I remember being struck by the very homeliness of it—the couches, the chairs, the paintings, the curtains on the windows, the sculpture, the writing table, the daybed—and, of course, the organ, at which the madman was now whirling about in astonishment, his concert interrupted by the onrushing arrival of our tidal wave.

As we spilled forward, he grasped Christine and dragged her through the doorway. Regaining our feet, we struggled after them. He must have toyed briefly with the idea of locking us in, but evidently changed his mind, preferring to put as much distance between himself and his pursuers as possible. Outside, we found ourselves on top of the embankment, running after them both, though to be perfectly candid the Vicomte by this time was barely able to move; I dragged him, even as the creature dragged her.

Nobody now leapt off the outer wall, pulling Christine with him, and they landed in a heap on hard-packed earth, the monster forsaking his hold in the process. In the next instant, Raoul, with his last reserves of strength, had flung himself off the wall upon his terrified mistress, and there he stayed, shielding her body with his own, his wound now reopened and pulsing scarlet.

The creature looked up at me, gauging his chances of recapturing the object of his all-consuming desire. Another shudder from above decided him, and he made for the earthworks in the distance, where I could see a trapdoor.

"Stop him!" I cried. "If he reaches the sewers, we are lost!"

The boy was in no condition to understand my warning and still less to respond to it. He would not quit the girl, and I saw that if the beast was to be destroyed I alone must accomplish his death.

I ran like a demon along the top of the embankment and hurled myself off the precipice at his retreating form, managing only to clasp him about the ankles as I crashed to the earth.

From the beginning I knew I was completely overmatched. My opponent fought with the savagery of ten men, and when I endeavored to apply the pressure points of baritsu, it was as if they did not exist in his anatomy. I might as well have been attempting to wrestle with an iron statue or a giant squid, for his arms seemed as lengthy and tenacious as tentacles. He clasped me about the shoulders and upper torso with such force that I felt the air being expelled from my lungs by pincers of steel. I contrived to throw a leg behind one of his and brought us both crashing down together once more, his hot breath steaming against my neck as though I were locked in mortal combat with the devil himself. His hands were now about my throat, and I knew that grinning death's head before my eyes was to be the last thing I ever beheld.

In a final act of desperation, motivated less by rational thought than any other act of my entire career, I tore the mask from his head.

Ah, Watson, the horror of it! In many ways the face I confronted inches from my own scarcely resembled a human visage at all, and that sufficient to stop the heart of a dog. There was no nose, only a mangled crater, and though it had two eyes, one bulged obscenely, almost dangling from its socket, while the other perpetually rolled upwards so that only white showed. The mouth, too, had been split apart, the upper lip curled back on itself and torn away, leaving only scar tissue and exposing irregular, snapping yellow teeth. Such skin as covered the whole was stretched so taut and thin as to resemble cracked parchment, for it was all cross-hatched with a delta of scars and patches. The crown, too, was bereft of all save a tuft of white hair that obeyed no brush but waved haphazardly aloft by itself.

But stranger and more dreadful than all of these were the sounds that issued from the throat of the Gorgon. Gone was the voice of indescribable beauty and in its place came a series of

squeals and grunts that would have done justice to a sow before the axe.

He recoiled in a kind of terror, his hands held up before his abhorrent features, waving like a pair of inarticulate claws, and then, suddenly no longer capable of combat, he dashed from me towards the trapdoor, some twenty feet from where I was on the point of expiration.

What happened next consumed but an instant out of the history of time. There was a sudden roar and the roof fell in all about us. As I lay helplessly upon the ground, tons of earth and water collapsed upon the poor, unfortunate Nobody. For the second and final time of his unhappy life, he was buried alive.

It was only by the merest chance that we three were not inundated simultaneously, but the bulk of the cataclysm missed us and we were showered instead with rocks and earth like a hailstorm from hell.

When the noise had abated, I was stunned to hear shouts overhead, and when I opened my eyes, I found I was looking up at blue sky. César snorted happily.

"Damnation!" exclaimed a voice from above. "That's three months' work gone for nothing!"

17

DIMINUENDO

*T*he sisters of mercy at the Hospital of Saint-Sulpice move in
miraculous silence. In their gowns of grey, their wimples, and their
enormous starched white headdresses, they glide soundlessly along
the endless corridors as if hidden under the length of their habits
were oiled wheels. They appear when needed as if by magic, and
their smiles, serene and grave, speak in silent whispers of the wonders of faith. Then, with a faint rustling, these exemplars of mercy
smoothly vanish.

I sensed the police hovering about my bed, anxious to renew
my acquaintance.

I was the first to be discharged from the hospital. I was as black-
and-blue as if I had spent the month in a meat grinder, and my
fingers were shredded by glass slivers, ending, for the forseeable
future, any thoughts I might have harbored concerning my future
as a violinist. Yet despite the privations and exposure I had suffered,

I seemed none the worse for wear. The assaults we perpetrate upon our fragile shells, Watson! I see you shake your head at the wonder of it. And yet these feeble bodies of ours still manage to protect our fluttering souls!

On this occasion there was no question about the phantom's body. At the same time members of the prefecture and emergency workers unearthed the six Algerian diggers who had been buried in the collapse of the tunnel, they also uncovered the corpse of the unhappy man who had led such a fantastic and troubled existence for so long in the bowels of the earth.

How could I have failed to recognize that insistent thudding as the jackhammers and steam shovels on the Rue Scribe?

As for the Vicomte, his wound was not a serious one, but the youth had lost a deal of blood, and it was deemed necessary that he undergo complete bed rest. The doctors counted on the young man's innate good health and normal appetites to reassert themselves and complete his recovery. His sanity, which had hung for a time in the balance, was restored by the sight of that individual who meant more to him than anything else in the world. Christine would sit next to his cot by the hour, never letting go his hand, even while he slept.

Her own mental condition revived at his touch, and so they stayed, clutching one another in a sort of mutual umbilical union, each taking and providing nourishment from the other.

It was several days before I had the opportunity of visiting with them again. In the meantime I was obliged to spend many hours in the company of Inspector Mifroid of the prefecture, who proved himself as tenacious as a foxhound in pursuit of his quarry.

"You will kindly begin at the beginning," said he, "and omit nothing, monsieur." He gestured to a secretary who held his pen at the ready.

There was nothing for it, Watson, but to tell him a large part of the entire business. His eyes widened and he tucked his chin into his neck with skepticism at hearing my name and I could see he was prepared to dispute me, but I soon set him to rights. A wire to Mycroft at the Foreign Office and various other assurances finally persuaded him of my true identity, and with some little difficulty I succeeded in extracting him promise to maintain the fiction of my demise. I did not share with him any of my experiences before my arrival in Paris, but confined myself to a history of the curious events which had taken place since my employment at the Opéra. Having discovered the corpse of Nobody, he now ceased attempting to shake my story, which was to a degree supplemented by the testimony of Ponelle, whose background in this area proved most helpful. That young man—along with the obstinate Bela and the rest of the orchestra—was now convinced that my placement amongst them had indeed been at the behest of the authorities.

"So you were telling the truth after all," he exclaimed, over a farewell coffee at our usual rendezvous.

"A tedious habit," I lied.

"They've patched up the Garnier vault, you will be interested to learn." He could not help grinning. "I promise you I shall remember our excursion for the rest of my days."

"I shall miss you, Ponelle."

"Just when I was getting used to your unorthodox style of bowing," offered Bela, who understood nothing of the reference to the Garnier vault. I daresay he would have denounced us both for blasphemy if he had. "We shall be sorry to lose you, Sigerson. I think even old Leroux had developed something of a soft spot for you."

"And I for him." This, as it happens, was true. There was something about the way the *maître* had conducted himself, so to speak, throughout the entire affair that won my admiration. His credo, so simple, so constant, and so laudable, in the face of all distractions,

shone with a kind of purity that excused a great deal of his tyranni-
cal presumption. He was a great conductor. I am not certain his
excesses would be tolerated in one who was not.

Mifroid, still in a combative humor, accompanied me with his
stenographer to the hospital, where we found the lovers much as I
had left them—the little Vicomte still asleep and his mistress yet
retaining her hold of his hand.

"Christine, this is Inspector Mifroid of the prefecture."

"How do you do, mademoiselle. Do you feel capable of telling
us the details of your ordeal?"

She cast an anxious glance in my direction.

"You must think me very gullible, monsieur." I smiled.

"Not in the least." I cast my glance in the direction of the
policeman, and she nodded.

"It was in this way, messieurs. I came to the Opéra that night
determined to sing. Monsieur Sigerson"—Mifroid, I was relieved
to see, made no move to correct her—"had encouraged me to do
so, having convinced me that my benefactor"—here she lowered
her voice to a reluctant whisper and made a rueful face—"would be
forced to show himself and thereby aid the forces of . . ." She hesitated again. What, she seemed to wonder, were we the forces of?

"Daylight," I supplied smoothly. She made a tiny gesture with
her head, signifying her acceptance of the definition. ". . . to cap-
ture him. Poor Nobody," she sighed.

"What do you mean by Nobody?" demanded Mifroid.

"He called himself by that name, monsieur."

Mifroid blinked in surprise at this but stuck to his mission.

"Please continue, mademoiselle."

"As Monsieur Sigerson instructed, I stayed well clear of my
own dressing room until it was time to go onstage. I was in the
wings, waiting for my cue, when I heard Nobody singing, and I very

nearly swooned at the sound of it. I thought I should die at that moment. There is—I should say there was—no other voice in the world to compare with it. The stage manager's stool was near where I stood, and I collapsed upon it and held my hands over my ears to stop that . . ." She searched for the right word, then shrugged to herself helplessly. "That impossible sound." She coughed, clearing her throat at the memory. "Then he walked off stage left, and I felt better. I knew he would be swallowed up by the walls before anyone could reach him, and this comforted me. My dizziness abated. During *Le Prophète* I made myself stand and walk about. When finally the curtain rose for me, I was frightened, but I concentrated. I remembered all he taught me"—she realized this now, with some irony—"and I sang as I always sang—for him alone." Tears formed in her eyes, but she blinked them resolutely away. "You were right, Monsieur Sigerson, the music sustained me."

"That is music's greatest virtue, mademoiselle."

"And then?" Mifroid pressed, with a transparent, oily obsequiousness that she could not fail to notice, but did.

"I took my bows and then I backed upstage. All at once everything went dark.

"At the same instant the ground opened beneath my feet and I was caught by a pair of iron arms. Before I could cry out, a hand was clapped over my face and I inhaled some sickly aroma"—her head twitched at the memory of it—"and that was all I remembered for some time.

"When I awoke, I was as one in a fairy tale or dream." She cast her eyes up towards the hospital ceiling as though the memory of what happened were written there. "I was sitting on a beautiful white horse, led by a tall chevalier in red with egret plumes. We descended by a narrow path all lit by a thousand candles until we came to a mist-covered lake. It seemed almost as if I were under a spell of enchantment."

"A lake?" snorted Mifroid, forgetting his former sympathetic pose.

"I know it sounds absurd. Perhaps I was still asleep and dreaming, monsieur."

"Well, it sounds as if you were."

I motioned him to be still. "Pray continue, mademoiselle."

"It was so like a dream," she repeated. "At the margin he helped me dismount and I slid again into his arms. He carried me as if I had no weight at all. I floated in his embrace." Here she cast an anxious glance at her lover, and then, recollected to her narrative by a cough from me, continued. "Now he placed me in a boat—"

"Bah!"

"Please, Inspector. Have the goodness to pay attention."

There was no need to urge Christine again. Her tale had acquired a momentum of its own, and her eyes glazed over, staring at nothing, while the story told itself.

"We rowed across the magic lake, parting the mist with our oars. It wasn't terribly far, and then he scooped me out and brought me to his house."

The memory of the house caused her to blink, in some way bringing her up short.

"It was a perfectly ordinary house with every sort of comfort. My room was ready for me—"

"*Your* room?" burst out the policeman. She nodded but did not look at him.

"It had clothes just for me, in my size, with my taste. Like Snow White. There was a bed, and there were some of my favorite pictures on the walls. The bookshelves included the Bible and copies of my most treasured volumes. There was a dressing table and a boudoir—all just as if he could read my mind and know every thing I craved. He had anticipated each of my desires." She had drifted

off again into the kind of toneless singsong that seemed to charac-
terize the narration of her dream. I wondered if this was one of the
lingering effects of the chloroform.

"At one end was a large organ with three keyboards and pedal
stops, and this he began to play, first giving me fruit to eat and a
glass of cold wine. He did not have to tell me what the music was. He
was playing his opera. You know"—she glanced at me briefly—
"Don Juan Triumphant, the one over which he had been laboring for
so long. I listened—it was magical—and he sang. And as I listened,
I was overcome in the strangest fashion, consumed with a desperate
yearning, all part of the dream, you understand—the dream I was
living. I stole quietly behind him, drawn by the music, but also
obeying like one in a trance some inner impulse that I could not
explain or deny." She hesitated.

"Yes?"

With her free hand, she mimed what happened next.

"I came up very softly behind him and then—swiftly and suddenly—I tore off his mask!" She gave a gasp and clapped a hand
over her own mouth, whether to stifle her recollection of the event
or to keep from waking her lover I could not say.

"He turned at once. Ah, that face! If I live to be a thousand,
how can I ever forget that face?" She turned to me for confirmation. "You know, Monsieur Sigerson. You saw." I nodded, but she
appeared not to notice, so absorbed was she in her own memory of
it. "But even stranger than the face, so distorted—even beyond
itself—with rage and surprise, was what came out of his mouth! No
speech, no beautiful voice, no voice at all, but instead a kind of
horrible squeaking! He fell upon the ground and writhed at my
feet, his jaws open, but the only sound they emitted was a series of
mewling cries and strangled—" She left off trying to find the words,
her mouth yawning open and shutting like that of a goldfish.
Mifroid watched, dumbstruck himself. "Finally he reached up-

wards towards me with a trembling arm. I knew then what it was he wanted; what he needed.

"I had the mask in my hand, you see. Automatically, I surrendered it to him. You would have done no less, had you seen him, pitiable as any crippled beggar sleeping under the Pont Neuf, but worse than the meanest of these, cursed with that face that would shrivel even the sight of a blind man.

"With a palsied hand he took the mask from me and with some difficulty succeeded in affixing it once more to his misshapen head. When it was secure again, it was as if his own self returned. He rose to his feet, steadying himself against the table first, then leaving it alone and swaying slightly before me, like a drunkard. I could hear him whisper to himself, testing, making sure his voice had revived with his false face.

"When next he spoke, words beautiful and sonorous came out of his mouth as of old, though his fury was terrible. 'Are you satisfied?' he cried, with a sound like a heart breaking. 'Now you have learned my secret! Are you *satisfied?* Do you know what it has cost me to have you see me thus, I who love you as the night adores the sun?' I trembled to hear these sentiments and knew not what to say. 'For days, for weeks, for years even, I have lived in my kingdom of perpetual night, wanting for nothing—*until I heard you.'* He choked on these words as a drowning man chokes on the water that floods his lungs. 'Until I heard you and my heart cracked like a bell with pealing your name.'

" 'What do you want of me?' I asked him in a whisper, sobbing for pity's sake but also because I was by now so terrified. 'What must I do?'

" 'My opera is finished,' he explained impatiently. 'As I told you it would be. It is the work of a lifetime. I wish you to perform it with me. Your voice alone will do my heroine justice.'

" 'And then may I leave?'

"The question appeared to surprise him. 'Where do you wish to go?' he demanded. 'Here is everything you could possibly desire.'

" 'When I told him that I wished to return to my home and Mother Valerius, he became agitated and stormed up and down the room. 'You are not being truthful with me!' he shouted. 'It is not the old woman whose caresses you seek!' When I insisted that after I sang, he must let me go home, he threw me on the bed and cried, 'Here is your home! Here you shall be my bride, my queen, and henceforward this shall be our domain.'

"As you can imagine, I was greatly frightened by this, for, having seen his features and listened to his ranting, I understood at last that my angel was a madman. He had indeed killed for my sake, and now for my sake, who knew but he might kill again?

"And all the while, there was a terrible shaking all about us, and he clenched his fists and raised them threateningly to the roof of his little home and bellowed like any beast of the jungle. Finally, I saw there was but one way to placate him, and I agreed to perform his opera."

There was a long silence. The Vicomte stirred again in his sleep, and, grateful for the interruption, she laid a fervent kiss upon his forehead.

"The work is not a short one and it took some time to sing, the more especially as its creator had such exacting standards regarding its execution, but I could see that my efforts soothed and fulfilled him for he appeared quite exalted to hear his music. I confess I found it to be as beautiful as he had led me to expect. But I continued to be so frightened that I was obliged to rest from time to time, a respite the composer granted me with greatest reluctance. All too soon he would become impatient and rouse me from my fitful slumber. So possessed was he by the need to complete the

performance that he was quite careless of my own fatigue and indifferent to my fears.

"Later, I heard a voice call my name through the wall," she said, tenderly stroking the young man's troubled brow until it smoothed again and a smile played about his lips.

"The rest, I believe, you know." Her voice by this time had subsided into a whisper faint as the evening breeze.

When she looked up at us at last, tears streamed silently down her face.

"Promise me, monsieur," she implored, looking directly at me. "Promise me he can never come again."

"Never again, mademoiselle."

Then she shook with convulsive sobs that I thought would last until the end of the world.

It was time for me to leave.

18

EPILOGUE

Sherlock Holmes knocked the ashes from his pipe and stretched his arms above his head. It was twilight, not *l'heure bleu,* but an old-fashioned English twilight, with a grey fog rolling in from the Channel and a chill replacing the vanished sunshine, which caused us to draw our chairs nearer the dying fire. Outside our windows was heard no more the happy buzz of apian activity but rather I fancied I could make out the distant pounding of angry surf.

"The Paris Underground, called the Métropolitain, opened in 1900. It isn't a patch on our own, of course, and they never did complete the line along the Rue Scribe—the ground was simply too unstable."*

*The Paris Métro in its original form may well have been inferior to the London Underground, but today it is generally conceded to be much superior, one of the great mass transit systems in the world. Many were killed digging in the treacherous boggy soil—as were many also working on the Toronto subway as recently as the 1960s, when cave-ins were the order of the day.

"Anyway, you stopped him," I said, piling my foolscap into an orderly stack. He laid a thin finger atop it and looked at me with bright, earnest grey eyes.

"Not I, Watson." He shook his head. "Not I. It was the twentieth century that killed the Ghost."

I sat for a time in silence, pondering the strange tale I had just heard, and formulating in my mind all the questions I wished to ask concerning it. Holmes appeared to be ruminating on the story himself, for he stared into the fire and made no move to leave, mesmerized, I take it, by the memories he had resurrected.

"Not my finest hour, Watson, as I am certain you will agree." He smiled and laughed that dry, silent chuckle that was typical of him.

"But you did succeed in rescuing Miss Adler."

"Yes," he admitted in a neutral voice, avoiding my eyes.

"What else?" said I, seeing him still in the thrall of his memories. He shrugged noncommittally.

"Of course, I went back more than once and prowled about the tunnel, searching and searching, but I never found it."

"Never found what?"

He regarded me with astonishment.

"Why, the opera, my dear fellow. *Don Juan Triumphant.* But the whole place had been smashed by earth and water and not a page survived." He scratched the back of his head in a gesture of regret. "What a pity. How I should like to have heard it properly. I have the strong suspicion it was a masterpiece." He shrugged. "Ah, but then, perhaps it was quite ordinary and I am merely being a romantic."

"You?"

"You needn't look so surprised, my boy. I was on holiday at the time. And in Paris." He rose and walked to one of the bookshelves, peering with difficulty at the titles in the gathering gloom.

"Ah, here it is." He pulled down a large volume and brought it over for me to examine. "This is all I did manage to unearth."

It was a copy of the *Iliad* in an English translation, swollen to twice its original size and heavy in my hands as though the water were still enhancing its weight. I heard myself sigh.

"What did you make of his reference to his mother?"

He shrugged.

"I cannot make anything of it. It certainly confounds a part of my theory—mine and Ponelle's," he added, smiling at the recollection of the young violinist. "If the creature's story about his mother is the truth, then our entire list of suppositions regarding his identity are in error and we can never know who he really was. It must, I fear, join that ever-lengthening list of unanswered questions whose combined weight incrementally retards the spinning of the planet."

"And the Vicomte and Mademoiselle Daaé? What became of them?"

"They married and lived happily ever after." He chuckled, aloud this time. "At all events, they married."

"That's more like the sentimentalist of my acquaintance," I said, smiling and feeling oddly reassured.

We were interrupted by a knock at the door.

"Beg pardon, Mr. Holmes," said Mrs. Hudson in a respectful undertone. "The Prime Minister is here to see you."

"Ah. I shall be with him presently, Mrs. Hudson."

"Very good, sir."

"You see how it is, Watson," said Holmes, after she withdrew. "First they send the Foreign Secretary, and when he has failed in his commission, they haul up their big guns. I must not leave Mr. Asquith skulking about my parlor."

"Why, what is it?" I asked, for clearly the matter must be mo-

mentous if it had brought the head of the government to the South Downs.

"Have you heard of Von Bork?"

"Never. Who is he?"

"A very jolly fellow, Watson," said Holmes, tapping me importantly on the knee. "A jolly fellow, who goes in for jolly, jolly English sport." His smile faded. "Great and terrible things are in the works, old friend. This Von Bork is a bit of sand in the cogs of big gears, and I take it he must be removed." He paused and heaved a sigh. "It will take some little time to run jolly Von Bork to ground, I fancy. And they will insist that I do it," he added, with another sigh. "Excuse me, won't you?"*

"But Holmes," I said as he approached the door. "Allow me one question, at least."

He hesitated.

"One question."

One question only! A thousand inquiries crowded my brain, each competing for pride of place. Who was the Ghost's confederate? Where and when did the Vicomte come to be wounded? Whatever had become of poor Plançon? There was one question, however, which jumped to the forefront of my consciousness and posed itself before I could express another:

"Where were you headed when you left Paris?"

Sherlock Holmes's eyes twinkled in the fading light as he stood there, half in and half out of the open door.

"Montenegro, old man. Montenegro."

It took me a moment to realize what he meant.

By the time I understood, he had gone.

*It did indeed take two years for Holmes to run Von Bork to ground. Full details of the case are to be found in "His Last Bow."

ACKNOWLEDGMENTS

Usually, at the conclusion of these pastiches, I am at pains to express my gratitude and admiration first and foremost for the happy genius of Arthur Conan Doyle, whose creation has brought so much pleasure to so many.

On this occasion, my thanks to Doyle must also be accompanied by an equal debt of gratitude to the man who wrote *The Phantom of the Opera*. Why Gaston Leroux's fantastic, absurdist masterpiece should be so neglected is quite beyond me—possibly the various movie and pop-opera versions have preempted publishers' perceptions of its value, which is wrong—but in exchange for borrowing it and improvising my own variations upon it, I felt it fitting to make Leroux the orchestra conductor, who could truthfully say that he was responsible for everything, that the smallest detail did not escape his attention. Leroux was apparently a big Sherlock Holmes fan, so it is only fitting that they got to meet.

One confession: Leroux states that the events he is about to describe occurred "not more than thirty years ago." Since his novel was published in 1911, that could mean 1881, a date not compatible with the Holmesian chronology. I therefore have given a loose interpretation to the words "not more than" and brought the action of the Ghost forward by ten years. I hope no one is too bent out of shape by this.

In addition, I am, typically, indebted to a host of Sherlockian scholars and theoreticians, chief among them the late William S. Baring-Gould, author of the first Holmes biography as well as annotator of the Clarkson N. Potter complete edition, whose chronology I have accepted without demur.

Two Holmesian reference works proved invaluable, *Sherlock Holmes and Dr. John H. Watson, M.D.: An Encyclopedia of Their Affairs*, by Orlando Clark; and *The Encyclopedia Sherlockiana: A Universal Dictionary of Sherlock Holmes and His Biographer, John H. Watson, M.D.*, by Jack Tracy.

I am also indebted to Otto Friedrich's chatty history of the Second Empire, *Olympia: Paris in the Age of Manet,* which fueled my interest in things nineteenth-century and French long before I dreamed of writing this book, as well as the Guide Michelin for Paris, which came in very handy after I had made the decision.

I owe particular thanks to my wife, Lauren, whose patience, advice, encouragement, editorial acumen, and unflagging enthusiasm kept me going when I became confused.

There is one final contributor who must be acknowledged.

"So your old man's a shrink," they said to me throughout my childhood. "Is he a Freudian?"

How was I supposed to know?

"Hey, Pop, are you a Freudian?"

"It's a silly question," he answered, lighting his pipe.

"How come?"

Acknowledgments

"Because you can no more discuss the history of psychoanalysis without starting with Freud than you can discuss the history of North America without beginning with the Indians—or Columbus. But to suppose that nothing has happened since Columbus is not only absurd, it is wildly incorrect. And it would be equally rigid and terribly doctrinaire to act as if nothing had happened since Freud."

(He then went on to present his mapmaking analogy with Columbus, which appears in the beginning of this novel.)

"When a patient comes to see me," my father continued, "I listen to what he says. I listen to *how* he says it. I try to hear what he does *not* say. Against these and other points of observation I apply a background of some clinical experience. I am, in short, searching for clues—*from him*—to help me determine why he is not happy. Freud doesn't much enter into it."

There was a long pause as I digested this. I watched my father puffing contentedly on his pipe. Suddenly I knew who it was that Sherlock Holmes had always reminded me of, all this time. I just hadn't been able to put my finger on it.

Thanks, Papa.